MW00582741

CORPORAL BOSKIN'S COLD COLD WAR

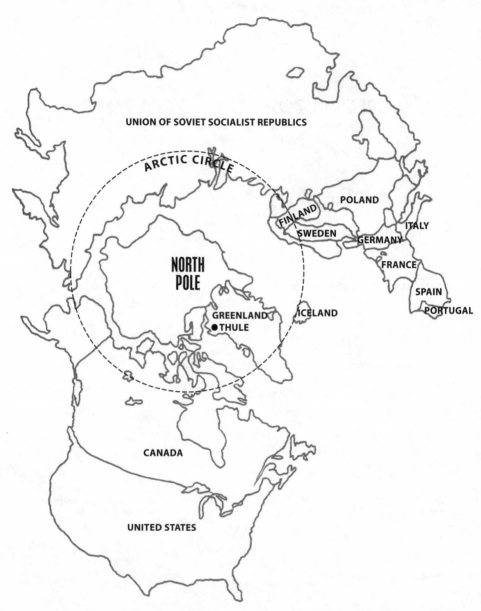

UNION OF SOVIET SOCIALIST REPUBLICS

ARCTIC CIRCLE

POLAND

FINLAND

SWEDEN

ITALY

GERMANY

FRANCE

NORTH POLE

SPAIN

PORTUGAL

ICELAND

GREENLAND
●THULE

CANADA

UNITED STATES

Map. Courtesy of Kris Waldman.

CORPORAL BOSKIN'S COLD COLD WAR

A Comical Journey

Joseph Boskin

Syracuse University Press

First Edition 2011

11 12 13 14 15 16   6 5 4 3 2 1

∞ The paper used in this publication meets the minimum requirements
of the American National Standard for Information Sciences—Permanence
of Paper for Printed Library Materials, ANSI Z39.48-1992.

For a listing of books published and distributed by Syracuse University Press,
visit our Web site at SyracuseUniversityPress.syr.edu.

ISBN: 978-0-8156-0964-3

Library of Congress Cataloging-in-Publication Data
Boskin, Joseph.
  Corporal Boskin's cold Cold War : a comical journey / Joseph Boskin. — 1st ed.
    p. cm.
  Includes bibliographical references.
  ISBN 978-0-8156-0964-3 (cloth : alk. paper)
 1. Boskin, Joseph.   2. United States. Army. Transportation Arctic Group.
3. United States. Army—Biography.   4. Thule Air Base (Greenland)
5. Cold War—Humor.   I. Title.
  U53.B67A3 2011
  355.0092—dc23   2011031745

Manufactured in the United States of America

David (1929–2010) and Michal Van Dommelen, whose artistry, individually and together, embraced and elevated all lives.

The best move lies close to the worst.

—Norman Mailer

JOSEPH BOSKIN is emeritus professor of American Social History at Boston University. His writings on issues relating to social and ethnic conflict include *The Oppenheimer Affair* (1968), *Urban Racial Violence in the Twentieth Century* (1969), *Into Slavery: Racial Decisions in the Virginia Colony* (1976), *Sambo: The Rise and Demise of an American Jester* (1986), and *Rebellious Laughter: People's Humor in American Culture* (1997). He was fortunately promoted to sergeant long before this current work appeared in print.

Contents

Illustrations

Acknowledgments

The shaping of this narrative was enriched by a motley crew of vibrant friends who reached out in ways gentle in tone and quirky in thought. I will always cherish their wraparound imagination and zesty playfulness: Mark Friedman and Ruth Chad whose laughing tenderness and linkage filled every day with togetherness; Mary H. Connor whose acute insights were always right-on; Sandi Olson whose touching clasp encompassed; Jason and Pat Finkle whose stream of banter constantly uplifted; Sheldon Benjamin whose sagacity was unerring; Allan Jay Friedman whose music proffered sweet nourishment; Michael Benari whose photographic third eye elevated; Michael and Kay Lunine whose universe connected all; S. M. Miller who prodded sagely, then prodded again; Donald Altschiller whose keen bibliographical knowledge plied the byways; Sam Fuchs whose broad expertise was invaluable; Trevor H. Kaye who plumbed the interiors with acuity; and, especially, Charlene O'Connor, whose eager intellect and sharp eye widened the possibilities.

Over the stretch of time, never-failing embraces from folks plus family sustained and succored:

David and Marjorie Kunzle, Larry and Kathy Roth, Damon and Marion Lawrence, Dorothy Kaufmann, Robert Erwin, Julian Troup, Lenny Quart, Deborah Gitell, Joe Nyomarkay, Marlene Flower, Yoav Benari, Arnold Shapiro, Dan Kuhn, Richard Tremaglio, Richard Weiss, Kristen Eichleay, Edith Loring-Thomas, David Maynard, Helen Jacobson, Richard Hynes, Constance Chesnut, Kathryn Kirshner, Selma Goldfield, Elizabeth Fox, Herb Boskin and Carolyn Webb, Claire Boskin, Mel Boskin, Honey Geyer, and Perry and Munjeet Geyer. Plus the soaring love of daughters-three,

Julie, Lori, and Deborah, along with Gary and Dan, together with Alyssa, Jonah, and Abigail.

Finally, preparation of the manuscript was particularized by marvelous individuals. A rarity is Mary Selden Evans, managing editor: Her zest for the story was heightened by imaginative direction and gracious lilt. Kelly L. Balenske, associate editor: Her multifaceted talents solved many a vexing issue. Mona Hamlin, publicity and marketing editor: Her ardent input expanded the horizons. And to the various divisions at Syracuse University Press: What a creative, joyous crew to have journeyed with . . . !

Cambridge, 2011

Prologue I

Thule Air Force Base, Greenland, 1953

Thule Air Force Base
Greenland 1953
SCENE 1

S E T T I N G

PLACE: Transportation Arctic Group (TRARG): Temporary Hdqs
TIME: Late April 1953, Midday
WEATHER: Biting cold, fierce winds

C H A R A C T E R S

COLONEL WALTER BALSTRUM, Commanding Officer, TRARG
PRIVATE FIRST CLASS JOSEPH BOSKIN, Historian

Subject: Pentagon Status Reports: Interoffice Memos

TO: P.F.C. Historian

> Last batch rpts not yet up to par. Yr ass still half-showing. Repeat: DO
> NOT offer any more than is required. But yr making progress. Keep
> up the good work.
>
> C.O.

TO: C.O.

> Thank you, Sir. I'll try to cover half my ass but still remain uncertain
> as to which half it is.
>
> Pfc. Boskin

TO: P.F.C. Historian

It's the half that reveals too much to the Pentagon.

C.O.

TO: C.O.

Sir, that half is shrinking so fast there won't be enough pertinent material in the rpts to report anything.

Pfc. Boskin

TO: P.F.C. Historian

I prefer butts that way. Know that I'm watching yrs carefully. I trust this is finally getting through to you so keep it covered, Boskin, all the way up.

C.O.

Prologue II

Boston, 2011

> History is not entirely to be believed but sometimes as they say you
> had to be there . . .

It was the Korean War, now referred to by historians as the "Hidden War,"
but I was nowhere near the front line, not even close to the 38th Parallel.
A case of severe myopia had propelled me to an alien place, specifically
Thule Air Force Base in northern Greenland. I was a twenty-two-year-old
draftee, a noncom, with the Transportation Arctic Group (TRARG), a top-
secret, scientific expeditionary outfit consisting of approximately three
hundred military specialists of all stripes plus a contingent of civilian scientists from the United States and other Western European countries. I
was the TRARG historian.

My Thule situation was, to put it mildly, intriguingly frustrating and
enlightening. After that military experience, I plied the historian's trade in
the theater of academia and never again came remotely near Thule. Yet, as
the whimsical adage declares about Brooklyn, you can take the soldier out
of Thule but not Thule out of the soldier.

The bizarre locale and piled-up contradictions, the company's Cold War
half-concocted mission, the struggle to sort out reality from fantasy, the trun-
cated Pentagon reports, the wrangling over the role of history, and the ultimate question of "was this really necessary?"—all of this has never vanished.
At a certain point came an urgent yen to set the record "straight," or perhaps
to set the episode "straight" as I perceived it—which is to say the reality of
what occurred skitters within the layers of animated and distant time.

Yet all this happened! There was this crucial mission: thousands of hours went into its planning and multitudes of specialized personnel were involved; countless curses accompanied its tortuous problems and endless hours were spent collating and writing a history; hundreds of millions of dollars were (ill-) allocated; and although not many bodies perished, there were persons maimed and several deaths. Disillusionment at the time, or thereafter, was impossible to tally.

Then, nothing. . . . It was gone, over and done. Conveniently forgotten between the chapters of the vast, volatile, variegated episodes of the Cold War. Yet, isn't this what prompted David Halberstam to get as much down as possible in his monumental *The Coldest Winter: America and the Korean War*? "For many Americans," lamented Halberstam, "except perhaps a high percentage of those who had actually fought there, Korea became something of a black hole in terms of history. In the year following the cease-fire, it became a war they wanted to know less rather than more about."[1]

Such refusal, however, slightly changed later in the decade. A few more works made their appearance, also in an attempt to sort out the episode that still has long-term repercussions. Prominent was Bruce Cumings, *The Korean War: A History*, which took serious umbrage with the conventional interpretation of the war's beginnings, the fighting itself, and the aftermath. Especially, Cumings emphasized that his input was "about a forgotten or never-known war and therefore, ipso facto, is also about history and memory."[2]

There was no actual fighting in Thule but the war was there, incessant, intense, and imminent.

Historical Tapestry

Built upon official military files, myriad personal notes, and recollections, plus scads of letters and materials proffered by my main buddy, David Van Dommelen, this tale about a miniscule, refracted slice of the Cold War is a verisimilitude history. Many TRARG files were lost or misplaced, still more were discarded along the way to the Pentagon, and more were destroyed in a flood that inundated my parents' tiny bungalow home when a hurricane raised the waters of Sheepshead Bay in Brooklyn.

On the positive side, Dave, who offered me his personal letters written to his wife Mike, plus a separate cache of papers purportedly written by me at the time, filled in many gaps. How he came into possession of these texts is part of the mystery of the mission but also of his surprisingly peculiar role in the military enterprise.

But of course there is more, not at the personal level but the highly technical, specifically the multivolume history of the mission itself that was finally declassified in the mid-1990s. Other smaller insights on matters operational also made their appearance to fill in gaps in the narrative.

So I have thoughtfully and caringly, though somewhat frolickingly, reconstructed the past. I console myself with the notion that history's recreation lies in the collection of facts reconfigured and elevated by one's idiosyncratic imagination. This narrative to "preserve experience" comports with the parameters of memoir built upon fact, recall, and expansion. As Mara Naselli has perceptively observed in *Truth in Memoir*: "It isn't that fact doesn't matter in memoir. It's that the very form, at its best, wrestles with the fact and the space between fact and fiction. Because there's always space between fact and memory. We are dependent on stories, not fact, to make sense of our lives. Our narration of a traumatic or life-changing event isn't created in the event. It's created in hindsight as we try to make sense of what happened, and like good storytellers, we amplify some things and recede others through a quiet sleight of hand."[3]

Fortunately, not all the notes in that bungalow drowned that day. And as I read and reread the remaining notes half a century later I recalled with some astonishment having compiled and written them. Sandwiched between the decaying papers, however, were several that defied recollection. They certainly sound familiar, as if I had written them in a rush. So I was jolted. So much for memory! Did I really write all this at the time? What if I didn't actually scribble all I thought I had? What if I had purloined the notes of another of my former TRARG buddies who was also hell-bent intent on soul-searching, exposure, or otherwise? What then? Well, then, surely, a story or two in this melded history reflects on both our parts, and my possible unintended plagiarism is reinforced by another's insight as well.

Isn't this what Michele Morano in *The Fourth Genre* lamented about, that such obstacles are a perpetual headache because of a constant gnawing to get things *right?* "Writing from personal experience and from memory involves negotiating with ourselves over every piece we write, grappling with questions of truth and accuracy and fairness, which is really hard."[4]

Intriguingly, E. L. Doctorow, whose keen thoughts and vast writings over many decades have shaped historical perceptions, carried this approach even further. In his essay, "False Documents," Doctorow maintained that "there is no fiction or non-fiction as we commonly understand the distinction: there is only narrative."[5]

I am nothing if not reverential about history. And these days I find myself railing even more than usual about the lack of historical consciousness in American culture, to say nothing about the utter lack of just plain, basic information that plagues.

Constantly journeying back into time, I often re-create its kaleidoscopic scenarios. A recollection projector located somewhere in my mind often triggers the on button, producing events sharply etched and others hazy that nonetheless refuse to dissolve into nothingness.

But there's another reason why I frequently summon up the past. Despite my occasional doubting the proposition, I believe in history's efficacy, that deciphering the past has to count for more than knowledge for knowledge's sake. Not to apply history is to insult it, denigrating those who grappled with its issues and problems in an attempt to decipher life's thickets. Directions into the future are obtained by determining the screwy turns of the past.

Still, even I was not prepared for a portion of my own history that entwined with the early years of the Cold War. When the Thule episode ended in the mid-1950s, it was over, finis, and I was not at all unhappy during the ensuing years that it got sucked into a black memory hole.

Then, in the mid-1990s, history turned a gnarled corner, and scenes from Thule rumbled back, triggering beguiling curiosity and comedy. Like so many at the time, I had not foreseen the ending of the Cold War itself, the beginnings of which had coincided with my own ongoing grappling with American foreign policy. Those years were so entangled that when the memory projector turned itself on and TRARG flickered onto the screen, I knew it was time to unravel the entire episode.

And an old cartoon became fresh again. Half a century ago I felt a kindred spirit with "Willie and Joe," the grizzled front-line infantry soldiers made popular by cartoonist Bill Mauldin during World War II in the Army publication *Stars and Stripes*. Of his numerous, bittersweet cartoons, one had really gotten to me. Mired in a foxhole half-mucked with water, Willie looks wearily at his buddy Joe: "You'll git over it, Joe," Willie exclaims with sad eyes. "Oncet I wuz gonna write a book exposin' th' Army after th' war, myself."

Like them, I wanted to expose a hidden segment of the early years of the Cold War, assuredly one of the most complicated periods in twentieth-century America. Bracketed by a repressive political atmosphere spearheaded by Senator Joseph McCarthy of Wisconsin on one side and unremitting terror highlighted by the possibility of nuclear war on the other, it was an era of intense vulnerability. Responding to the dual threats, the national government and various states responded by setting up nuclear bomb shelters, instituting loyalty oath programs, clamping down on "subversive" groups, scouring history textbooks for their "unpatriotic" statements, and cleansing public comedy of satire and spoofing. The resultant anti-intellectual zeitgeist, observed by the outstanding historian Richard Hofstadter in *Anti-Intellectualism in American Life*, fostered a heady social climate of "fervent malice and humorless imbecility."[6]

Nonetheless, the challenge of the Soviet Union was fraught with dark possibilities, and Thule Air Force Base was a major linchpin in the strategy of containment designed to squeeze tight the enemy. TRARG was designed to test equipment, with a longer view, I came to believe, to peer into the possibility of constructing yet another Thule, way on the other side of Greenland but hundreds upon hundreds of miles closer to Moscow. Was this latter mission really necessary, was it that critical, to seek out the construct of yet another air base capable of demolishing the enemy?

The stuff of this particular scenario is told in the embodiment of the familiarly termed "narrative nonfiction," though personally I prefer historical tapestry. Commingling reality with imagination, it offers the scope of memoir fleshed out with enlivening images of what occurred. The overriding pursuit here is a verisimilitude history, a re-creation intended to

"You'll git over it, Joe. Oncet I wuz gonna write a book exposin' th' Army after th' war, myself."

1. Willie and Joe cartoon. Copyright 1945 by Bill Mauldin. Courtesy of Bill Mauldin Estate LLC.

underscore the inclusive thought of a writer who once proclaimed of such nonfiction: *What does it truly mean to be human in such circumstances?*

In this context, real names are largely kept while certain others are altered in the hope that the characters and events, actual and extended, resonate true. There is no intent to undermine or slur anyone who was involved in this military journey. Anthropologist Roger Abrahams carried this notion to a relevant place in historical drama: "Anytime somebody tells a story about something he did which involved a kind of extreme action, or mysterious or traumatic event, all kinds of details have to be added to justify it, to make it more profoundly dramatic."[7]

TRARG was but a flyspeck in the history of the Cold War. Who except scholars pay homage to such miniscule episodes? So steeped in historical abstention is America that the majority don't give a hoot, anyway. Nonetheless, as a metaphor of might, Thule Air Force Base and TRARG surely mattered at a particular historical juncture, and even in this new millennium, its embers still inflame. The mission still offers up the shrift of historical magnitude.

Sanitized History

Back in the states at the conclusion of TRARG's operation in 1953, I participated in compiling a two-volume, top-secret report for the Pentagon. The final contents were in the hands of the Commanding Officer; it was his proverbial ass that was on the line.

More recently, in the midst of weaving this narrative, a wonderful librarian friend called to inform me that the multivolume TRARG report had been declassified. Several weeks later I was literally fondling yellow, decaying pages, poring over material familiar yet so distant. Perusing them after many decades instantly rekindled seriocomic spleen. I had forgotten how bemusedly mortified I had been back then when the report was being formulated. I was once again ticked off: it was, of course, the Colonel's story.

These final volumes are excruciatingly detailed, legitimate solely in their advancement of Arctic technology. They offer virtually nothing contextual, nothing about the significance of Thule Air Force Base, and especially nothing about TRARG's task in exploring the possibility of widening the military playing field. There is nary a passage about the brio and frustrations of a top-secret outfit wrestling with human and topographical obstacles in their quest to carry out a special mission. It is, sorrowfully, sanitized history.

To be sure, TRARG was tiny but its mission far-reaching, an outfit whose top-secret objective was matched by equally far-out costs commensurate with the Cold War policy that anything goes to undo the enemy. Its portal of operation began at Fort Eustis, Virginia, then moved to Thule AFB, a linchpin in the Strategic Air Command nuclear bomber strategy, and then further onto the vast ice cap. Our merry band of career and draftee specialists were in the thick of history, whether we realized it or not.

Introduction

This tale has a beginning, but no ending . . .

The beginning was the draft, in 1952. It was the second year of the Korean War, referred to as the "forgotten war," when tens of thousands of men were being inducted monthly into the US Army and US Marine Corps.

I was no more, no less, than any of those beefing up the military in the intensifying, overarching Cold War. Having just graduated with a master's degree in history and political science, however, I wound up as one of the few soldier historians in the military. Degrees aside, I was a neophyte, with only fervor and humor making up for deficiencies.

At the time, the Pentagon was organizing an especial wartime outfit: a top-secret, expeditionary, scientific group, the Transportation Arctic Group (TRARG), for several objectives in Northern Greenland. Its major operating base was the mammoth Thule Air Force Base itself, but the unit constructed lesser camps along the edge of the ice cap. The company consisted of 275 men, regulars and draftees, as well as a cluster of civilian scientists from the United States and other European countries who at various stages worked clandestinely with the outfit. And at various times during TRARG's experiments, a slew of investigating congressmen eagerly arrived to jump aboard the whirling helicopters that soared over breathtaking glaciers.

Throughout the 1950s and into the 1960s, Thule Air Force Base was shrouded in almost-total secrecy. A white metropolis, the base was monumentally costly, a brilliant engineering feat and a linchpin in the global containment policy designed to prevent another sneak attack on the United States. Flying time over the Greenland ice cap was a scant five hours to the heart of the USSR.

Every day / all-day / year-in-and-out / before missile weaponry was developed, B-52 bombers loaded with thermonuclear weapons took off, and headed to pre-coordinated targets throughout the Soviet Union. Unknown to most Americans, Thule was shrouded in mystery but the enemy knew . . . Russian MIGs equipped with cameras came as close to the base as possible before fighter jets catapulted to intercept and destroy them when possible.

TRARG-at-Thule had as its ostensible purpose the testing of equipment and mapping the treacherous terrain onto the ice cap. But there was a desperate, covert yearning beyond the surface: It was to determine the feasibility of constructing yet another air base on the other coast of Greenland, one that would be much closer to the enemy.

At the conclusion of TRARG's mission, a multivolume report was literally frozen deep in the top-secret vaults of the Pentagon and remained entombed there until being officially defrosted almost a half-century later. As detailed as the final reports were, they contained barely a smidgen of the human episode itself, none of its daily comedic breathing, the entwining characters and their anxieties, the inner scope and space of activities, the near and actual losses, and the poignant interaction with the Inuits, whose village skirted the base's outlying boundaries. Nor did it include the ongoing tug-of-wills between the company commander and his private-first-class historian, soon elevated to corporal, over the nature of the status reports sent weekly to the Pentagon.

This seriocomedic account of TRARG, its top-secret mission and its personal dimension, hopefully fills a gap in the enormity of the Cold War. A mixture of plot and memoir, there are factual shortcomings and crevasses. Not all the occurrences can be verified, nor are the conversations exact, plus some of the names have been altered. But for whatever this is worth, the storied past can be presented as verisimilitude history.

PART ONE

May 1950–February 1953

The Place

Thule Is the Spot

For Ice, Snow and Mountains
Thule is the Spot;
Battling the changing weather
In the land God forgot.

For here the Men of the Army,
Working hard for our pay,
Guarding millions of people
For two-and-a-half a day.

Here's the ice and blizzards,
Here's where a man gets blue,
Down between two mountains
Three thousand miles from you.

The freezing cold, it comes and goes,
Almost more than we can stand;
No, we are not condemned convicts,
We are defenders of our land.

No one knows we are living,
No one gives a damn,
Lock, stock and barrel
We belong to Uncle Sam.

Living with our memories only,
Hoping to see our gals,
Praying that when we return
They're not hitched to our pals.

Here we sit with our radios,
We listen till we are sick;
Then back to work we go
Too damn weary to kick.

Then comes the day when all good men of Thule
Will go to a place known well,
And St. Peter will say, "Pass Through
You men of Thule:
You've served your time in Hell."

Thule Air Force Base, Greenland
Author(s) Unknown

1

Defying the Tundra

Dawn of a Base

The unraveling of this military yarn begins in the early 1950s when two men, an Inuit and a Frenchman, were on their way back from the ice cap to the village at Thule . . .

Huskies Recoiled in Every Direction

"Takou. Look!" Touching the shoulder of the French explorer, the Inuit pointed to the horizon. "Takou. Look!" Unexpected yellowing orange clouds of dust were billowing over North Star Bay. Jean Malaurie grabbed for Outak's binoculars. Short, punctuated white vapors in the cold air rose from shocked breaths.

Swiftly descending the slope the two came upon "a spectacle that I thought must be a mirage," wrote Malaurie in *The Last Kings of Thule* in 1956.[1] On an Arctic plain that "only yesterday" had been stark tundra landscape were skeletal shapes and forms of an emerging city of steel frameworks, huge hangers, blacktop runways, oblong aluminum living quarters, and an assortment of low buildings. The two men just stared, wordless. "Astonishment became stupor," Malaurie exclaimed.

Uninterrupted, incessant roars from the huge yellow Caterpillars pushing tons of boulders and excavators with elephantine jaws biting into the small mountains raised plumes of dust. Zigzagging jets and helicopters jostled Outak and Malaurie, forcing their imaginations and exclamations. And "the huskies, more used to the bear than to this strange din," recoiled in every direction.

3

"Thousands and thousands of Americans," exclaimed Outak hoarsely to his villagers upon his return home, "you can't count them. They come every day from the skies. And there's the atomic bomb too. We Inuit have been here a thousand years. We certainly thought that 'Toullay' was an important place on the earth . . . Now they say that they are going to heat the sikou, the sea-ice, to make it melt. There will be almost no more winter. Then they'll send us to the North Pole," he exclaimed anxiously.

Outak suddenly had an inspired insight about these new, strange people. "Aah! We understand it all now. None of these Americans have got women. It's not normal, that. Sofia heard that they wanted our 150 girls. Poor things."

Work on the base continued at a frenetic pace along with mounting uneasiness between the Thule Inuits and the American workers. Crouching around a piece of seal, Outak and his villagers talked about the new taste of meat mixed with chewing gum. Massive gasoline leaks and industrial wastes, propelling seals and walruses away from their habitats, never to return, eroded the purity of inlet waters. "All that," said an old man,

2. Thule sign.

his finger pointing to Thule base, "all that is not for us. Nothing good will come of it."

Mayonnaise

The Korean War was raging atop the glowering embers of the Cold War. More than 55,000 men were being drafted each month. A diagnosis of severe myopia in my case did not in the least deter the Pentagon. Deferred for a year while in graduate school, the draft board in Coney Island had refused to extend my civilian status any further. Then came the US Government's letter in fall 1952, which as every draftee knows, begins with the winsome salutation "GREETINGS," immediately followed by an explanation intended to offset ire: "Having submitted yourself to a Local Board composed of your neighbors." Exactly which neighbors? Even at this distance: their names, please!

The Cold War was then in its early furies, and I wound up in an orchestra seat, not in the front rows but close up, enough. Along with two hundred seventy-five men, plus a batch of scientists from four different countries, I was in a polar universe, a US Army top-secret, scientific expeditionary force ordered to Thule Air Force Base and the adjacent Arctic ice cap. I was the outfit's scribe.

Those assembled for this open albeit clandestine operation possessed an uncommon mixture of expertise, half being regular army, officers and noncoms, specializing in mechanics, engineering, operational management, medicine, and an assortment of highly skilled crafts. Only a few of the noncoms had gone beyond high school, and many had been in the Second World War.

The other segment, draftees, had just completed college, with master's degrees in cartography, geology, glaciology, geophysics, botany, and electrical and mechanical engineering. Rounding out the company were the administrators, the so-called pencil pushers, who were in both groups.

Regulars and draftees, this was an oddball mix of origin and age imbued with its separate views of time and intent. We had been thrown together in exceedingly tight quarters on a two-pronged mission: to wrestle and conquer the trickiness of Greenland's terrain as it ascends and descends the ice cap; and then for the Pentagon to determine the feasibility of constructing, on the other side of the continent thousands of kilometers away, another base even closer to the USSR.

Despite President Harry S. Truman's 1948 executive order integrating the armed forces, TRARG was the color of mayonnaise, and maybe just as well because many of the regulars who hailed from Texas, Oklahoma, and Arkansas made no bones about their intense dislike of blacks. This was 1953, a year before the Supreme Court decision in *Brown v. the Board of Education* and several years before Dr. Martin Luther King Jr. guided the bus boycott in Montgomery, Alabama. Close contact in the cramped quarters of Thule and the ice cap would have resulted, I strongly feared, in guerrilla racial warfare. A smattering of New York Jews was about as far as the Southerners were willing to go. Not that they had any choice in the matter, but their ethnic boundary line was elastic only up to a particular point, provided its numbers were miniscule.

Eager to apply my chosen profession, I had actually volunteered for the outfit. Contrary to military folk wisdom of never, ever, making oneself visible to higher-ups, I had applied for the historian slot in the Transportation Arctic Group. Equal parts of logic and madness went into the making of this decision. Singularity plus curiosity, the rare chance to be the sole manuscripter of a moment in historical time. I would be able to scribe an unvarnished story.

Or so I thought.

Perversity has its own take on things, however. Here was an enterprise that offered round-the-clock sunlight, a view of iceberg births, and treacherous crevasses, plus the ice cap itself. Here was a chance to peer at miniature trees, tiny flowers, and miniscule fish. Here was an opportunity to view polar bears, walruses, seals, and arctic terns, and hopefully an Eskimo or two. And, here was the soldier's patriotic impulse to serve one's land. None of this of course was even remotely in my wildest imagination at the time.

How considerate of my government to expand my horizons, a Brooklyn boy from Coney Island and Brighton Beach growing up during the Great Depression, to be sent atop the world. Prior to college, I had never been west of the East River or south beyond Staten Island.

There was only one slight hitch. Despite its so-called designation as a top-secret base, by 1953 Thule was not an unknown quantity to the USSR military command, who were also keenly interested in the Northern Hemisphere. Flight over the North Pole brought us uncozily closer to each other, so to speak, in hardware terms. So they, and we, had built powerful air force bases in the Arctic region.

It was cold fission in the Cold War.

2

Prisoners of Our Time

The *H* Is Silent . . . So Was the Woman

Thule, also Tule or Thula, is an ancient term from the Latin, literally "farthest possible limit." The *h* is silent. To the Greek geographers, Thule referred to regions of the inhabitable world. Throughout antiquity, the ostracized were sent to an "ultimo tule," one of God's desolate, forsaken places, such as the isle of Britain. Wherever it was actually located, it was "a land at the edge of the maps," as Joanna Kavenna noted in *The Ice Museum.*[1]

As explorers over the centuries gradually filled in the geographical gaps, Greenland's northern slope eventually came to be known as "Ultima Thule," the phrase designated in 1910 by the Danish anthropologist and explorer, Knud Rassmussen, as an advanced post for polar expeditions.

Yet long before the explorers had made it a chief stop in the dogged quest for the North Pole, the locale was an active village home of Inuits. Their existence had preceded the Europeans by several thousand years. Nonetheless, it was precisely at this spot, on a spit of land adjacent to a harbor and fjord where massive ice pushing downward from its center thunderously spawned menacing icebergs, that the United States decided to build a most powerful complex—in terms of dollars and energy one of the most costly. Expectedly, it was named Thule Air Force Base.

When I arrived in the early spring of 1953, there were approximately four to five thousand men, and one woman, not exactly a healthy recipe for any kind of social arrangement. Greenland was then part of Denmark, and the United States had arranged a ninety-nine year lease on the Thule region, and this sole, isolated, hardy person was the wife of the Danish

Liaison Officer. Her reputation at the base was a grim joke: "She's the world's wealthiest woman!"

Reality was another matter. The liaison's house was strategically located in the middle of a vast, open tundra field and guarded around the clock by the Air Force Police packing submachine guns. Passing the binoculars back and forth we would watch *her*—"the world's most beautiful, wealthiest woman!"—as she gazed at the endless sky or hung out the wash on circular lines or played with her two children and husky dog. Once, peering through the glasses, I thought she spotted me as she herself scanned the terrain through her binoculars! I tried to wave, felt stupid, and half-held back. But she raised a waving hand high! Did I get it right?

I was elated, then thought: we are both prisoners of our time.

Naturally, the subject of women was always at center stage in Thule. Several French scientists who arrived in midsummer animatedly inquired, "Where are the whimmon??" A finger pointed to the sole female off in the distance. "Mon Dieu," came their instant reply, "you Americans are barbarians!"

Years later, a medical company consisting of WACs (Women's Army Corps) eventually came to Thule, too late for my company, and in any case the officers, as they always did, would have deep-frozen us ordinary soldiers, if you don't mind the pun. The next time we encountered women was upon our return to Fort Eustis in the fall, a memorable occasion when a group of WACs raucously welcomed us back to Virginia civilization.

Base Boondoggle

There is a finely tuned quip in the military: "Don't ask why!" There has never been a truly rational answer as to why the US Army decides anything, like, say, assignment to a particular place or a military occupational specialty. I trust to hell there never will be. At this stage of life I have no desire to relinquish my axiomatic faith connecting military logic with random chaos theory.

My younger brother, Mel, for example, drafted six months after I was, had studied the taxonomy of parasites. At the height of the Korean War, the military was in desperate need for this expertise. What happened to

him? Instead of Korea, he was groomed as a small-parts equipment spe-
cialist and shipped to Trieste, Italy. Immediately after disembarking from
the troop ship, the sergeant at the dock asked for someone who could type
more than twenty-five words per minute. My brother's hand instantly
shot up. He was a klutz as a typist but knew the score. Within minutes,
despite all that specialty training, he wound up in charge of the Noncommissioned Officers Club, an arrangement that complemented his education and the Army's need because, as he pointed out, all sorts of profligate
parasites bred at the club.

In my case, I had just completed a master's degree in American history
and political theory. Somewhere in the vast regions of military bureau-
cracy someone decided that the best place for a myopic twenty-two year
old with such esoteric degrees was Fort Eustis, the US Army Transportation Center.

Located in the Tidewater region of Virginia, the area is dear to historians researching the emergence of American democracy. Jamestown,
Yorktown, and Williamsburg constitute the historical landmarks, as did
plantation slavery—but that went unmentioned in the local brochures in
1952 or, for that matter, in the welcoming speech to young black and white
basic trainees forced to tour the colonial attraction.

Named after a Civil War general of no major consequence, Fort Eustis
was located in a terrain that made absolutely no military sense. A slew
of military camps had been built in rural areas throughout the South,
offering up marvelous examples of congressional boondoggling. Here in
a swampy, humid terrain, miles from anywhere remotely connected to
transportation outlets, was the center of the Transportation Corps. Here
bodies were trained as jeep, truck, and amphibious landing-craft drivers
and helicopter pilots, plus low-level stevedores.

No, Fort Eustis was hardly the ideal location for a transportation
center but it certainly suited a particular insect. Breeding merrily in the
Tidewater's ecology was the malaria-bearing mosquito that for many centuries had bitten and dispatched many a colonist, regardless of sex, race,
creed, or color.

Was the US Army aware of this deadly chronicle? Of course! Aircraft
filled with tons of DDT attacked the base every spring. Plumes of white

powder descended from the heavens, blocking out the sun, while the troops remained indoors for hours. Just prior to this health purification drive, hundreds frantically placed plastic covers over their cars to prevent the chemical from corroding the paint. Normality returned shortly afterward, and we walked and paraded on the fields covered with DDT. Shoes, socks, and lower trouser legs became covered in a dirty white film shuffled into the wooden barracks, offices, and off-base homes.

Here was where the "Arctic Group" trained for its top-secret mission to northern Greenland.

Long before I arrived, Fort Eustis had already been dubbed *Fort Useless*.

"Tell the Motherfuckers"

This was the time of early racial integration, as President Truman's Executive Order had eliminated apartheid in the military just a few years earlier, in 1948. More or less, anyway. The base was a classic study in selective racism: blacks as jeep and truck drivers and stevedores; whites as helicopter pilots and administrators; more blacks as noncommissioned trainers; and almost all officers white.

The surrounding locale, by contrast, was totally mired in segregationist practices. With both *Brown v. the Board of Education* and the Montgomery bus boycott still in the offing down the civil rights pike, Jim Crow laws iron-cast the terrain.

So I shuddered, when halfway into basic training the company commander called me into his office and pointed to "historian" on my record and said I was "the ideal person to lecture on the colonial period of Jamestown, Yorktown, and Williamsburg." Revving up patriotic fervor was part of basic training, and basic trainees at Fort Eustis were obligated to tour colonial Williamsburg, the cradle of American democracy, so the brochures exuberantly declared.

Most of my company went ballistic. Blacks, mainly from New York and New Jersey, balked at going, exclaiming that Williamsburg is segregated from top to bottom and they were not about to be "fucking insulted." Joining in the protest were other New Yorkers, largely Italians and Jews. I posed the company anger to the company commander. His response was unequivocal: "All troops will assemble at 0800 and all troops will visit Williamsburg, where American democracy began."

Entering the lecture hall at the tourist center there was a noticeable bristle in the ranks. As we filed past the racially designated drinking fountain and bathroom signs, "Colored" and "White," guys openly hooted. The small auditorium, filled with soldiers and a handful of tourists, was decked out in colonial bunting.

At the lectern was a middle-aged woman in colonial dress that cheerfully invoked the political wonders of colonial Williamsburg. I was then introduced by the company commander as a bona fide historian the Army was proud of having in its ranks. Slowly heading for the stage, a treacherous thought plunged straight to my tongue: what *in hell* am I doing here? To my relief, my tongue managed to extricate itself from the thought. "Hey, Boskin," a black guy in my squad shouted as I was about to begin, "tell the motherfuckers where it's at and let's get the fuck out of here." Sitting in the front row, the commanding officer stared straight ahead.

3

At the Creation

Historical Objectivity!

It was January 1953. The post of historian was way, way down on the list of specialists ranging from helicopter pilots to cartographers to glaciologists to electric engineers to mechanics to carpenters to radio operators to clerical administrators posted on a special announcement for a brand new outfit, the Transportation Arctic Group, 9223rd Technical Services Unit. I was then the personal secretary to the officer-in-charge of basic training at Fort Eustis and privy to all secret and top-secret incoming operational information.

TRARG was conceived by the Pentagon as a scientific, expeditionary force consisting of military and civilian experts from the United States, Britain, Denmark, and France. Flitting in and out during the operation would be high-ranking Pentagon observers plus traveling congressmen. The ostensible objectives: to test equipment, map the terrain, and achieve other related technical ends. Hidden, however, and only gradually revealed as the layers of operational trials stealthily unfolded was a larger scheme: a grandiose leap in military base positioning.

About the position of historian itself I felt brashly capable. About Greenland I knew nothing save what I had learned at P.S. 225, namely that "Eskimos" survived in the frozen near-nothingness, pictures of their dark-skinned, smiling-eyed, walrus-clothed bodies etched against whiteness. The place had absolutely no relevance to my concrete streets and stoops of Brooklyn, with the occasional exception of a heavy snowfall that led to snowball fights and sledding blessings.

According to the operation's format, the historian's task was to collect weekly status reports from all the various units, regardless of where they

13

were operating, detailing their progress and problems and collating them in exacting military language. A summary account was to be immediately forwarded to Colonel Walter Balstrum, the C.O., who after putting his own touch on the batch would transmit it to a Special Operations office at the Pentagon. Upon the completion of TRARG's mission, they expected a full, major history.

None of this perturbed me. At this stage, not knowing the tricky intricacies of the military system and overloaded with brashness, I was elated at the prospect of compiling and writing a history of a top-secret mission. What did perturb, however, was that as an observer and participant in the episode itself I was violating a basic precept that historians hold most precious to their work: distance. How could I maintain cherished objectivity while directly involved in the unfolding drama itself? As it turned out, this issue was rendered a nonproblem early into the operation when the C.O.—not a historian but something more important in the higher realms of life, a career officer—provided his own definition of "historical objectivity."

(Another aspect unnerved, though this wasn't too serious. While my command of grammar was passable, it was my good fortune that the C.O.'s was even lousier.)

Then there was the question of hierarchy. Given the military's rigid separation, would being a private first class hinder when it came to dealing with the officers? When the C.O. sent word down that the historian's deadlines were to be rigidly met, there was much grumbling but compliance. At the same time, there were those who were as acutely mindful of their own careers as the C.O. who viewed *me* as the true enemy.

I sat down in a sparse, tight office as a stern-eyed officer, my files open before him, pointedly questioned my military intent and overall purposes in life. Why had I applied? How far along in my academic degree-career? What did I hope to achieve as the historian? What were my politics? Did I plan to leave the military when my two-year draft stint was over? And, oh yes, did I have any questions? I decided to ask innocuous ones and then get more exact, but after my very first inquiry he closed my dossier and stated that within ten days I would be informed whether I would be in the outfit.

Within a week after arriving at Thule, my education as historian began in earnest with a metaphorical snowball. Before the Pentagon ever laid eyes on a single batch of reports, the C.O. pointedly retouched and embellished the unit's weekly achievements. "AAAhhh, to ensure objectivity, Private Boskin, keep that in mind!"

"Sir, as a historian may I offer a point about objectivity here?"

"AAAhhh Boskin, what're you quibblin' about?! Objectivity is in the mind of the beholder, don't you agree!" He was about six feet two inches tall but appeared much larger with outstretched beefy hands and arms. Brainy and articulate, he had the bearing suitable for high command and rarely failed to impress. Approving my promotion in mid-summer to corporal, he cheerfully repeated his directive, chuckling on the title he had just conferred. "Remember, Corporal Historian, the rank from which you just came, a return trip is not impossible. And bear in mind the next promotion down the road. So continue in the ways of objective history!"

The C.O.'s snap stuck. Within short order Corporal Historian became common snide fare among the officers who came to hate the status reports. "But Sir," I would patiently intone either on the phone or in their makeshift offices or in their going up or coming down the ice cap, "the C.O. needs your report on time, it's for the history." The ice cap was a stretch of snow, massively ranging from one coast of Greenland across to the other, ten thousand feet at its height, tapered at both ends by open and submerged fissures in the terrain: dreaded crevasses.

History: the very word made them shudder if not choke, and the fact that their reworked progress reports were being forwarded to the Pentagon didn't make them any friendlier. It wasn't long before they balked at the demanding weekly deadlines and took to hiding. When eventually I tracked them down in some tundra or snowfield, eliding effusions greeted me: "It was a good week, Corporal Historian, aaahhh, yep, yep, much done, much accomplished, a damned good week." Behind their wan smiles was "so fuck off you twerp, this is all you're getting."

Slightly deterred, I remained convinced that by writing between the lines to fool the C.O. and whoever else, I could pull off a bone marrow history of a small outfit writ large in the Cold War itself.

Was I wrong . . .

Cozening Up to the Enemy

Again, just what was the US Army Transportation Corps doing atop the world? What was the ultimo purpose of assembling this extraordinary group of military and civilian specialists and technicians at *Ultimo Tule*? It grew out of the obvious recognition that Northern Greenland was crucial in a war with the Soviet Union, the air route to Moscow a mere 2,772 nautical miles away, barely a five-hour flight.

Plans to protect the United States in the upcoming confrontation with the USSR were concocted in the early 1950s. Within several years the Pentagon had ordered construction of a major weather station on the ice cap, about 800 miles from Thule, as part of the Distant Early Warning (DEW) complex, the early alert radar system that circled the globe.

Constructing the radar station itself was a monumental engineering accomplishment. Given the ferocious weather matched by treacherous terrain, plus the lack of Arctic experience, it was amazing that the effort got anywhere. Problems like crevasses always surprised. The first attempt ended just fourteen miles outside Thule when tractors and equipment in a heavy sled detachment broke through a series of invisible snow-bridged crevasses. Nobody expired on that occasion but it was a stark reminder of such a possibility. The radar station remains in operation to this day.

TRARG's task was infinitely trickier. Its major objective, openly detailed in the official documents, was to explore the feasibility of locating safe pathways onto the ice cap by locating and managing the treacherous crevasses along the way. Crucial to the entire operation was developing the capability of hauling tons of cargo and multitudes of men onto and then over the ice cap, ten thousand feet at its apex, and undisclosed in its design, figuratively sledding down to the other side. None of this was possible unless and until myriad technical problems could be deciphered, then solved.

Just getting onto the stark ice cap was a tormenting task. Sudden storms plus innumerable, shifting crevasses blocked easy access. Some faults were effortlessly observed, others concealed under shaving-cream surfaces; crevasses run to short depths or plunge to oblivion.

That's what accounted for the unusual mix of civilian and military scientists from four different nations. TRARG's research division was "entirely new in concept," wrote the Pentagon designers, "the rather unusual integration of a civilian group into a military body required not only a sufficient erudite understanding of scientific tasks but a considerable amount of tact and demonstration of good will."

What the Pentagon hungrily wanted was another major air force base cozening up closer to the Soviet Union. But what they were not yet fully aware of was the enormity of the undertaking. So many immense problems confronted virtually every snowy step along the way. An armada of tracked vehicles carrying men and supplies sailing across a frozen white sea to the ice cap ten thousand feet at its apex and then down to Greenland's eastern edge, a sea visible only when the fiercest of winds didn't obliterate the sky, the plan was awesome in design and monumental in logistics.

No one possessed any illusion of safety. Every military man and civilian scientist knew the story of two French scientists in a weasel that

3. Command Weasel.

4. "Heartthrob" Weasel.

toppled into a crevasse in the previous year, their bodies never recovered. It would have been near impossible to retrieve them in any case, but their families requested no effort be made as a symbolic tribute to their work.

TRARG's task was to pinpoint the crevasses by experimenting with electronic gear, or any other method that might work, and map the region. Those directly involved with this part of the mission took immediate advantage of the military life insurance plan.

Overall, then, this was an immense undertaking, an unparalleled one, emphasizing in military lingo TRARG's dual function "as a developing and user agency." Solving all these technological complexities required building from scratch an administrative base of operations at Thule Air Force base as well as a primary jumping-off site at the edge of the ice cap, dubbed Nuna Takeoff Camp. And if all this were not daunting enough, lesser posts around the fjords also had to be constructed. Inasmuch as there were just so many days of daylight, so many hours of tranquil weather, these interdependent objectives had to be accomplished *muy pronto* in the quixotic land of Ultimo Tule.

Huptwo, Hupthree, We Train Merr-ily for Thule . . .

Special training for this top-secret mission atop the frozen world was jux-
taposed against the singing spring of the eastern tidewater region.

At that time, when darkness covered the Arctic region, light illu-
mined the Virginia countryside. Up there, temperatures below zero kept
all solidly frozen; down in the south rising temperatures thawed out frozen buds. Thule's aching winds made outside work nearby impossible;
Fort Eustis's wafting winds liquefied bodily joints.

Greenland, then, seemed as remote as to be a figment of one's childhood imagination. The connection between Thule and Tidewater was
whimsy perched on a limb. "North" had no reality on anything except
for the shortage of time between assemblage and departure. Transport
to Thule was scheduled within six weeks—despite the fact that the outfit
was not yet fully complemented—which dictated an unimpeachable logic
that a particular kind of training had to occur at top speed.

Logic, however, is not exactly the military's forte. No sooner had I
been transferred to TRARG than the army's lunacy machine got into high
gear. During the Second World War, the term *snafu* was a regaled term,
yet never had I analogized the military as a loony bin rivaling the best of
them: *situation normal, all fucked up* apparently applies to all wars.

High-level training for the Arctic certainly occurred but only for a
select few. Several small groups attended courses in survival, equipment,
maintenance, medical operations, and similar uncertainties. The rest of
us, however, sauntered around a moth-eaten area somewhere at the edge
of Fort Useless.

Of course, then, the very first task assigned to this newly organized,
top-secret, expeditionary force designated for departure to Northern
Greenland in six weeks was to scrub spotless the decrepit barracks TRARG
had been temporarily shoveled into. Built in early 1940s, mothballed since
World War II, the army couldn't give away those dank wooden buildings even to Goodwill Industries. Crucial weeks swiftly evaporated as a
squinty-eyed major in white gloves inspected and then reinspected, scrutinized and then rescrutinized, anally and reanally fingering the grime
forever embedded in its cracks.

Then, to create the requisite discipline required to tackle the mission's exceptional scientific and technological experiments adjacent to the North Pole, we paraded! Endlessly, around and around, over and again, across the hardened dust fields until "You Men Get It Right!!" At first, the regular army guys whose careers dated back a full decade or more, elite specialists all, marched very grumpily, and then they softly disappeared into the hidden crannies of the camp. Quick learners by the third week, we draftees took up the cue. The officers frantically went out on scouting parties, muttering loudly about court-martial.

The chicken-shit cleansing and parading slid to a stop. And the lectures began. Slides, slides, more slides. Three weeks remained.

4

Little Rhody

Paul

Absurdity became the crazy glue of camaraderie. One moment a patch-work of strangers, then a pastel of conspirators. Scheming against the system immediately bonded. Strategizing to avoid the scrubbing, the marching and slide watching, became a hilarious game. Disappearing into the cricks of the base, frolicking on forged passes, the remaining short weekends eased the anxiety of unpreparedness. And by this time it was understood that the challenge, no more and no less, would be revealed as on-the-job training itself.

"The stupid-ass, fuckin' brass," laughed Paul Cavarotti from his bunk next to mine, "they sure know how to create instant enemies." He was particularly cheerful because in a few days we were off to the WAC Officers Training Base in mid-Virginia on a double date.

Our backgrounds comically coalesced, both of us coming from work-ing-class neighborhoods that were ethnically dense. Neighborhoods wound up tightly like a watch, the difference being that his town in Rhode Island was cozily tiny, whereas mine was cozily huge. Recount-ing my Brighton Beach street many decades later, I tallied up over nine hundred people squeezed into that small block. I had gone to Abraham Lincoln High School, located in Coney Island, which itself numbered in the dizzying fifty-five hundreds.

Comparing sizes brought us to laughter. My high school graduating class was almost the size of his entire high school. Rhode Island, I quickly learned, was a homey postcard that every resident read. As the lyrics of the University of Rhode Island school song went: "We're Rhode Island born and we're Rhode Island bred, and when we die we'll be Rhode Island dead." Yet there were the recognizable connections. Paul had prowled for girls in his beat-up car hooting along Main Street; I prowled for girls cruising on the boardwalk. He had worked at the local hamburger drive-in; I worked at a local luncheonette. Rendering our Italian and Jewish styles down, we nicknamed along geographic appellations: RI Paul and BB Joe.

"Shush, Queenie Might Hear . . ."

One night after the lights clipped off at 9:20, we got around to fathers and mothers. Paul came from an Italian family that brimmed with brothers and sisters; I was the oldest of three brothers. His domineering father was a lathe operator, swearing uproariously but drawing the line with his wife, the acknowledged "Madonna" of the household. My controlling father, a plumber and hustler, caroused playfully with his cronies but drew a strict line with "Queenie." Household language in our respective households was as pure as our mothers were.

It wasn't until my seventh year that I discovered my mother's real name was Diana, and her position constantly sanctified: "Never, *ever* talk back to Queenie!"

Shortly before departure to Thule, I snuck home on a purloined weekend pass. By coincidence my brother Mel, drafted six months after I was, was also home on pass. He had just completed basic training and had been ordered to the army's equipment depot, in Maryland. We were both in uniform dress.

Around the table for dinner, our younger brother Herb viewing us with awe, the conversation banter was about the comings and goings of relatives. Keeping with the practice long strictly set by our father, we sons cleared the dishes from the table. Talking while whisking plates, I sloppily tilted several dishes. Knives and forks clanked noisily on the floor. "Oh fuck," I said nonchalantly, bending down to retrieve them.

"*What* did you say!" exclaimed my mother.

I had not paid a whit of attention to what I had blurted out. My brothers burst out laughing. Not my father, whose eyes silently scowled.

"What?" I said to my mother, puzzled.

"That kind of language is out of place here. I don't care how old you are. Kindly do not use such words in the house."

"Oh, for Pete's sake, Mother, all I did is say fuck."

Brother Mel could barely contain himself.

"Joseph, there you go again!"

"Mother," I said exasperatedly, "the word is used in the army for everything under the sun, and I mean everything. It's practically in the army manual."

"Well, maybe there but not here . . . not here."

Mel came to my rescue. "Hey Mom, Joe is right, that word is used all the time. It doesn't really mean anything at all. It just means fuck, that's all."

My father's palm hit the table. But he was clearly amused. "Hey," he said, chuckling, "Queenie doesn't know anything about such things—and I don't think she wants to start now. So put a lid on it."

As he drove us to the subway, my father sidled up slyly, "Okay boys, wherever you go, watch your asses." To which Mel shot out, "You mean our fuckin' asses." "Shush," he whispered, "Queenie might hear."

Sandi

We had met in freshman year, in Oswego. Spotting her in a theatrical production, I was instantly enslaved. Flowing auburn hair, deep-green eyes dancing between high-freckled cheeks, a no-nonsense stride, she simply snared my imagination. We dated, stayed together, split. I spiraled into gloom when she gravitated toward others and despite relationships of my own always desired her.

Graduation came, and away we both went, she to graduate school at the University of Chicago, and I to enroll at NYU with a draft deferment. We remained in tight correspondence that was short-circuited by my father who intercepted, and trashed, her letters. My mother was intent on us not marrying.

Sandi surprised me soon after I connected to TRARG. Her call startled. She had enlisted in the WAC's Officer's Training Corps and was in basic training about forty miles away. Why would she do something like that? After mulling it over I finally made sense of it. An orphan raised by nuns, and then the next six years adopted by a Jewish couple, Sandi had always been on the run, always on her own. Fiercely free-spirited and anchorless, she had chosen yet another path to wherever it took her. I had always wanted to be her anchor. Now it was too late.

Fearsome MPs

Who knows how, but my private first class brother had access to blank weekend passes. He mailed up a batch. I distributed them around to my new buddies. A wiseacre sergeant complicitly filled in the necessary spaces. Thinking of Sandi rippled my mind. Paul had access to a car on the post while I now had access to Sandi and her buddy trainees.

I telephoned her and arranged a date for Paul. All was set for Saturday the week before departure. Exhilarated, Paul and I jumped up and down like teenagers invited to a forbidden party.

Narrow roads bordered by budded-leafed trees led into the camp. We were immediately struck by the sentry stares of guards, all women. Entering the headquarters building to check in, a granite-faced duty officer glared at us. It was the very first WAC officer we had directly faced in our short army stint. Keeping her unblinking eyes glued to us, she picked up a telephone and made a curt call. Silent minutes surrounded us before they finally emerged, meek and soft-voiced, sharply saluting the duty officer.

Sandi looked radiant but much thinner. Her bouncy hair was military shorn, her green eyes deep into their sockets, smile quieter. Yet she also looked as if she was in her element. I wanted to rush over and hug her. No fucking way. The hard-nosed officer continued looking directly at Paul and me while filling out the passes. She then admonished, "All right, you two, these girls are due back at 2200 hours, not 2201. Otherwise they're in deep trouble and I'll make sure you guys will suffer. Understand!" She paused, half-grinned at her underlings, and rang out, "All right, have a good evening, girls!"

Reality Checks Out/Reality Thunders In

Where to go posed a problem since we had no knowledge of the terrain. Nor did Sandi and her sister grunt. Tooling a short ways out of camp was a big red barn with a flamboyant neon sign flaunting the hottest country music anywhere. Paul and his date were delighted. Sandi and I, locked in embrace, couldn't care less.

The place was cavernous. Everyone was bouncing and whirling beneath a rotating mirror whose rainbow colors scattered all over the room. We scooted to a corner table and tuned it all out. A country-western band we could barely hear was blaring heart-wrenching songs. The table was small but Paul wanted no part of us, and it was mutual. And it all seemed so damned rushed, anyway. Even if we had wanted to catch up, it would have been impossible. We locked together, danced in tiny circles, and said little.

Her arms tightly encasing my neck, Sandi suddenly half-glanced at her watch. "Oh my god, we're due back in forty minutes." "Can't be!" I exclaimed. "Fucking time!" She rushed over to the table. "Rosemary, let's get going. Now—NOW!" We raced to the car.

Pulling into a dark space adjacent to the headquarters building, fifteen minutes remained before curfew descended. Paul and Rosemary yanked each other down in the front seat. Sandi and I were already halfway to the floor. Half-undressed in the narrow space, rushing oblivious to time, reality had checked out.

Reality swiftly thundered back in. The roof of the car was being bashed, and somebody beamed a sharp light through the window. GET-UPGETDRESSED GETGOINGNOW reverberated into the still night.

"Holy shit!" yelled Paul. We all jerked for our clothes, arms and legs flapping into each other. Whoever was doing the ordering had the voice of the Lord. When I finally got my glasses on and wedged back into the seat I saw a frightening sight: silhouetted against the light beams of a dark-green car were menacing figures in olive uniforms with white armbands and stark white helmets. "Ohhhhnoooo," moaned Paul, "WAC MPs!"

Six Degrees of Rhode Island

"All right, GIRLS," snapped the taller MP throwing open the car door, "it's past curfew time, so y'all in deep trouble." The girls bolted for the building. I think Sandi threw a sharp, rueful glance back but I wouldn't swear to it. There were white helmets above a white light in my eyes. An enemy unspecified in the warfare manuals had clearly ensnared us. Down the road, though, the infraction didn't prevent Sandi from departing the military as a colonel whose unusual specialty was photojournalism.

No sooner had the cowed trainees disappeared behind a thudded door than the MPs ordered us out of the car. Stationed on either side of us, light beams still in our faces, an eerie scene jumbled my mind. Thousands of tiny droplets in the dew-lit night melded the trees and buildings. Car lights, flashlights, barracks lights divided the night into serrated layers. For a split moment I was in the middle of an impressionist painting except for those long fingers pointing right at our heads.

"All right . . . who . . . the . . . *fuck* . . . are . . . you . . . *guys!?* I wanna see some papers, quick-like," said the shorter one, in cadence. Paul blurted that we were on weekend pass, and we handed over our forged authorizations. She turned them around ever so slowly. I prayed that our wiseacre sergeant hadn't fucked up because the MPs were just looking for some infraction.

"Okay," she exclaimed abruptly, thrusting them back, "they're in order. But you guys did something real bad—and I mean *reeeaaaalll* bad! You got these girls in deep shit because they violated curfew and they're going to pay for it—and so're *you two!* We're putting you on report."

Report? Whatever in hell did that mean?? It sure didn't sound too good.

Neither Paul nor I said a mumbling word. We had been too jolted by the turn of events. The whole scene was mesmerizing. I just kept blinking. Taking stock of our captors, I suddenly thought they looked pretty attractive, particularly the shorter one. Paul managed a plea. "Hey, wait," he said shakily, "hold on a minute . . . can't we . . . ?"

"Did we tell you to *speak!*" retorted the taller WAC. Paul's mouth froze in mid-sentence.

By now I was getting back from denial, so I picked up Paul's words. "Can't we—why can't we say something?? Don't we have right to say something! For one thing, we're about to SHIP OUT!"

That got them. "Ship out? To FECOM [Far East command]??"

"No, not Korea, not that bad," I replied, "but a place much colder, like try Northern Greenland!"

"Northern Greenland??" The shorter MP looked over to her partner, puzzled. "Greenland?! Are you guys putting us on?"

"Fuck, no," said Paul, "in a little over a couple of weeks we're on our way to some godforsaken place called Thule. Thule . . . Greenland! Can you believe it!? The North Pole's a hop and skip from there."

A sympathetic tone crept into their eyes. "How in hell you guys ever get assigned there?" asked the taller figure. "What's up? What's up there??"

Ratcheting up the compassion level, I invoked the secrecy gambit. "Sorry," I said as conspiratorially as possible, "we can't tell you anything because it's top secret. And we're on orders not to say anything, to anyone. But that's why we forgot about the time. We're not thinking straight these days." I hoped this would get us off the hook. It almost worked.

"Yeah, all right," replied the taller one, "I can understand where you're coming from—but there's something you're not getting . . ."

"What's that?" I asked.

"That, soldier boy, is that you two kept the girls past curfew, and they'll pay for it. Technically they're AWOL . . . that's what. You guys put them in that situation. So you guys have to be reported for causin' them trouble. Got it?!"

Paul's feet were shuffling back and forth. I could see he was getting really miffed. "Okay, yeah, but, why, tell me why they have to be punished at all. For Chrissake, it was only a few minutes. We just forgot about the time. They're not to blame. And we're sorry. We are!"

The MPs shot glances at each other. The shorter one slowly shook her head. "Well so's we, buddy boy, believe me, so's we. But we don't have much choice in the matter because the Duty Officer probably's already recorded the time and when the C.O. sees it on Monday she's gonna raise the roof. So let's get on with this. Let's see your driver's license."

Paul just stared at her, then reached into his back pocket for his wallet. It was now getting damp from the mist, soaking our heads and sweaters. Paul ran his hand through his hair to get rid of the wetness and handed over a moist driver's license to the taller one. Wiping the card on her armband, she told us to get back into car. We did as told.

Beaming her flashlight on the card she brought it up close, then handed it over to her sidekick with an uh-oh look. Uh-oh, I thought, Paul's license is expired and now we're really in for it, we're on our way to some stockade. The shorter one looked at it and then made a beeline to Paul. I couldn't imagine what she was up to. Is this a stolen car? I shuddered.

Holding the card and squinting down at the license plate, she let out a delighted shriek. "Are you from *Rhode Island!*" "Yeah," said Paul nodding. She yanked open the door and asked, "What town're you from??" Paul got out of the car, a big grin on his face.

Thank You O Lord for Creating Little Rhody

"From Point Judith," said Paul. "Do you know where that is?"

"Do I know!" she continued cheerily, "I'm from Galilee."

"No shit!" Paul replied, "I mean, yeah, that's right next door."

"Which high school did you go to?"

"Nashville High."

"What year?"

"1950. And you?"

"Me too," she giggled. "Did you know Sue Somolli?"

"Do I know Sue Somolli? Hell, yes, I dated her for about a year. Just how do you know Sue?"

I couldn't believe what was happening. Back and forth they went questioning each other, homing in on names, dates, events, whooping glee with each discovery, until they were practically kissing cousins.

In the meantime, the taller MP had gone into headquarters barracks and I slid further into the car seat and closed my eyes.

Fifteen minutes later Paul got back into the car, started it up, and blew a kiss to the MP. She waved merrily back. Off we went in the sultry night back to Fort Useless. He was whistling.

"Okay," I asked groggily, "what the fuck was all that about?" He didn't respond too quickly, just kept on whistling. "Hey, Paul . . ."

His eyes on the road, he murmured breezily, "Joe, you won't believe this 'cause you only think you know my state. Little Rhody just saved our asses. And what's more—what's more . . . is that I've got a date next weekend!"

"A date? What? You mean . . . with that MP?"

"Yup."

"How the hell did you wangle a date with her?"

"Like I told you, you've got to know Little Rhody. Everybody in my state knows everybody else. The place is just one big family. Eileen and I criss-cross in a dozen different ways."

"Eileen? Her name's Eileen?" I felt like an idiot repeating myself but I was tired and a bit amazed by the sudden turn of events. One moment we're in deep trouble, and the next we're home free. "What's her family name?"

"Mazerotti. Yup, another Italian. And would you believe her father's a lieutenant colonel in the Engineer Corps—at Ft. Belvedere in Maryland. Get that—a fucking colonel. I even know some of her cousins and she knows some of mine. Hey, she's pretty cute, don't you think? A great smile—and I bet underneath that wacky uniform she's stacked."

I thought for a moment. Sandi! Next week! "Hey Paul, why don't we make it a double?"

"Joe," said Paul deliberately, as if he knew my feelings were going to be hurt, "no way, I'm sorry but no way—no way."

"But . . . why not?"

"Joe, the whole situation works against it. First is the infraction that'll prevent Sandi and Rosemary from going anywhere for a long while. Eileen just told me she'll make sure that they'll be reprimanded, but nothing more serious. Second is that Sandi's a trainee and Eileen's higher up. No mixin' here. And if that's not enough, Joe, good buddy, I'm really interested in this woman and I want to spend time with her, a-lone, before we ship out."

No Sandi! I felt awful. When will I ever see her again?

"Paul, how'n hell are you going to fly the company coop again next weekend? All the blank passes are used up."

Paul laughed. "Hey, no sweat! Eileen's brassy father is gonna make all the necessary arrangements." He went back to whistling.

I slumped back into the seat.

A year later Paul and Eileen were married in one of the grandest weddings in the history of Little Rhody. Their invitation arrived just as I was returning from a stint on the ice cap. Paul was nowhere near Thule. Since they couldn't envision Greenland as their honeymoon, Paul's father-in-law had him transferred to an outfit in EUCOM (Europe) before shipping out.

They honeymooned in Venice, not California, Italy.

5

Ezekiel Saw the Wheel Way Up in Thule

If They Build It, You Will Be Ordered There . . .

"Now listen up assholes, otherwise you're in for a hard time, and somebody might get killed, and after a short while some've you will wish you had been," said the top sergeant with a mixture of contempt and amusement.

"Ohfuckoff," whispered Dave, my evolving main buddy.

But was the grizzly man right on target! The vista in early March was stunning, at once exhilarating and foreboding. Sandwiched between craggy icebergs still encased in an ice-locked harbor, and a range of dark low-lying hills flanking its sides, was Thule Air Force Base. The monstrous transport plane we had been crammed into plopped squarely onto the narrow-ribbon runway, cut its four roaring propeller engines, and for the first time in the three-day flight we could talk to each other without yelling. Yet so plugged were ears that we could barely hear any sound. Virtually half the company, together with tons of scientific equipment, trucks and tracked vehicles, ground its way down two stories into the Greenland dusk. Swirling icy winds carved into our cheeks and noses. From springtime Virginia to springtime Greenland, the cold morphing had begun.

Bewitched, bothered, as the song goes, and bewildered, we were all alike in reaction to the air force's reception. No sooner had we de-planed than the security police checked our identification papers, an act instantly regarded as paranoid. Maybe they knew something we didn't. But how or who in hell would or could want to sneak into an army specialized outfit bound for Thule?! A Russian spy disguised as a draftee?! Then when the officers were whisked off to posh quarters without their papers being

31

scrutinized, we recognized the scenario. Stupid-assed discipline, again. It was only the peons who were being treated suspiciously. This was quite logical, we draftees reasoned, inasmuch as officers are too fucking dumb to be spies.

Herded into a mammoth hanger, we listened to a tough major deliver a fierce lecture on secrecy: NO PICTURES OF THE BOMBERS!! NOTHING IN YOUR LETTERS ABOUT THE BOMBERS!!! NOTHING!! NOTHING!! DO YOU HEAR ME!! NOTHING!! We looked around—no officers at the orientation either.

Thule was the northern capstone of a global military complex that boxed in the USSR. It was also part of the DEW radar line that was strung across the world monitoring Soviet air actions to prevent an unforeseen attack. B-47s, later B-52s, armed with thermonuclear weapons, swiftly flew in and almost as swiftly departed from Thule, joining other bombers from bases around the world every hour, every day, every year to prevent, and then if it came to that, to instantly retaliate.

White Metropolis

Truly a magnificent feat, this Thule, this Air Force Base, rivaling any engineering creation in history. Operation Blue Jay was the designated code name given by the Pentagon in January 1950, setting in motion the building of this powerful military operation. Naming the venture after a bird, a harbinger of spring, was cutesy Pentagon public relations supposedly obscuring its overall intent. But there was no way the cognomen deceived the Soviets. How could it have been otherwise?

Within a few short years, Thule became more than an air base; it was an architecturally innovative white metropolis.

Stealthily mobilizing approximately 7,500 skilled male workers in Rosemont, Minnesota, waves of massive cargo planes carried them to Thule. Many others arrived on ships in July and August after the icebreakers had smashed their way through six feet of sea ice in Wolstenholme Fjord in Thule's North Star Bay.

Enticing the workers were fabulous wages increased by double-, even triple-time pay. Their skills ran the gamut from the prosaic to the finely honed and included chefs, laundry men, engineers, musical instructor, and restaurant manager. Most were veterans of previous global construction operations in Okinawa, Guam, Alaska, and Central America. They busted their asses—nothing much in Thule to distract anyone!—catapulting the workers into the burgeoning post–World War II middle-class.

For the earliest ones, though, it was a white nightmare. Sans wives, children, and friends, only the unrelenting schedule offset the physical and psychological grimness. The sun could be spotted above the horizon from 24 April through 21 August with total darkness from 22 November through 29 January. During the winters only an hour or two was open to any kind of exertion as temperatures of –40 centigrade degrees were not untypical, winds howling at 240 kilometers per hour keeping the cold cold. Even when not in use, engines were run nonstop to prevent them from freezing solidly. Workers bopped in and out of shelters for warmth before venturing out again. The winds never ceased so cables were rigged between buildings to prevent bodies from being blown across the frozen tundra.

Even worse was the lack of fresh water. Until a plant for distilling fresh water from salt was completed, everyone was dependent on melted ice that was so abnormally hard that any kind of washing was a chore. For this reason mess trays had to be scrubbed four times. After the distillery came into operation the water couldn't be piped because the tubes froze. It was delivered by truck, barrack to barrack.

Except for the short summer months when the powerful ship icebreakers, the *Eastwind* and *Westwind,* penetrated the thick ice, finally prying open the harbor for cargo convoys, every piece of equipment had to be flown in and the personnel out. Working at breakneck speed over eighteen months, there emerged an air base capable of demolishing the enemy. By summer 1952, almost twenty thousand workers, military, scientists, congressmen, and senators had come and gone from the area. Save for a few international cities, Thule was one of the most active airports in the world.

The metropolis itself had a cinema, library, restaurant, hospital, baseball field, gymnasium, Guffey's Tavern, fully stocked PX, massive laundry operation, and the largest distillery of seawater in the world. The radio tower was higher than the Eiffel Tower.

Items vital to modern urban life—from Band-aids to powdered milk to automobile parts to cotton gauze to hammers to toilet paper to pool balls to trucks to gasoline to soup ladles to boot polish to toothpaste to mattresses to typewriter ribbons to musical instruments to barbells to aluminum pipes to flour to packages to cameras to operating tables to nail files to shaving lotion to screwdrivers to booze to earth shovels to strawberries to soap to sunglasses to caskets to toothpicks to perfume to tickets to you name it—were shipped thousands of miles, mainly by huge cargo aircraft.

Still, it was all labeled a "secret" but on occasion "an open secret." "We don't even officially know where we are," the engineers and scientists told Malaurie, the French explorer who later ventured onto the base. "We are forbidden to tell our families, though some evenings we hear Radio Moscow talk about it. Then there are all those who go home at the end of September when their contracts expire, and the Danes in the village and working at the radio station—we can't shut their mouths. It's an open secret, I tell you, and sooner or later we shall have to talk."

Wherever TRARG ventured, security was thrown in our faces. We were warned about "small talk," about conversing too freely with the civilian workers, sending back photos of our various activities or about our letters detailing any of TRARG's experiments. A slew of predictable directives poured forth from the secretary of defense:

> In view of the general international situation and the continuing military in Korea, there exists the clear necessity of affording the utmost protection to our scientific, technical, and military advantages. The expenditure of lives and of the wealth of our citizens in the present defense effort makes it mandatory to ensure that our military secrets are not dissipated.

Military "secrets" not dissipated!? Soviet MIGs shuttling back and forth to Thule Air Base from their Arctic air base, high altitude cameras scrolling away, made a mockery of the word.

Moscow Molly and Leningrad Lenny

Descending and mysteriously departing, the thermonuclear bombers, like the Danish woman, were naturally under constant surveillance by armed guards and secret eyes. Unauthorized personnel, meaning us Thule warriors, were kept at a far distance. Lighted signs emphatically declared that cameras were strictly off-limits, a restriction reinforced by the security people who kept repeating that no pictures were permitted, and if caught snapping a single frame, well, then, prepare for the worst: a solitary hike on the ice cap, a summary court-martial, or for that matter, both.

Yet in September 1952, eight months before TRARG's arrival, *Life* magazine—one of the most popular photo journals in the country—had published an extensive seventeen-page article, "Birth of a Base," proclaiming Thule as a Cold War marvel. Sharply etched photos of the mighty bombers perched on the forbidden runways plus a detailed layout of the base were included in the piece! Guys in my outfit were startled when I showed them the magazine, and rightfully furious. Sarcasm replaced future discretion: "Hey, our cover is blown!" "Hey, now we're really at the mercy of the enemy!" "Hey, it's totally understandable—the Russians and the Pentagon—bosom buddies! They can both go fuck themselves!"

In reality, we had begun to suspect this from the moment we turned on high frequency transmissions and picked up Radio Moscow, which

5. Thule vegetation scaled by ordinary matchbook.

constantly harangued about Thule's "imperialist aggressors." Several English-speaking announcers, dubbed Moscow Molly and her cohort Leningrad Lenny by Thule's old-timers, gleefully informed that "the third light on the runway is broken." Such detail, needless to say, slightly unnerved. So they too had pretty good cameras! About the only group kept in the dark before *Life*'s spread were the people in the world's most self-proclaimed democracy. Despite the obvious duplicity, it was intended to be kept that way.

Finalizing It Frozen

Arctic terrain is layered permafrost, a shortened term for permanently frozen soil. Impervious to anything short of a nuclear blast, an amazing transformation occurs once the sun bores down on its surface. Under the sun's constant rays the permafrost eventually softens into mucky quicksand.[1]

Small rivulets produce miniature trees, diminutive yellowish and red flowers, tiny fish, and fiercely equipped mosquitoes. Consequently, in the early stages of construction, the runways, hangars, and housing units were precariously perched on the surface. Soon foundations began to crack, the hangars and runways sliding sidewise into the gooey ground.

Problem: how to ensure hardened topsoil that would keep the buildings and runways intact? The solution: levitation. The engineers raised high the structures. Atop wooden frames went long aluminum buildings. The buildings were fabricated like huge meat freezers with air piped in through the miles of interconnecting tubes, these also elevated on wooden stilts. It was life on a planet in outer space.

But the hangars, taxiways, and runways couldn't be placed on stilts. The solution: refrigeration. Tubes crossed underneath every few feet keeping the temperatures permanently permafrosted.

Another question that bedeviled the architects was the limited availability of open land between the harbor and the ice cap. Problem: how to provide enough room for all the bombers, transport carriers, fighter jets, and helicopters? The solution: separation. Raised, separate hangers and runways were constructed for each of the fighter jets, with a catapult underneath. With the front and back doors simultaneously swinging open, the combat-ready jets were instantly thrust thousands of feet into the wild blue yonder, similar to takeoff on aircraft carriers. After a while, listening to the schuussing sounds, we could estimate the number of planes being sent aloft to combat the enemy.

Aircraft, the lifeline to the States, the lifeblood of the base, was always at the mercy of the weather, which shifted, changed, plunged, often on a minute-to-minute basis.

Thule was a place of hazard and vulnerability, of wonder, and surreal, a scenario not to be believed until you finally got it. Or, rather, it got to you . . .

PART TWO

March 1953–July 1953

Thule and Nuna

SCENE 2

PLACE: The Three Ps Tent (Pencil Pushers Palace)
TIME: Mid-June, late night
WEATHER: Quiet wind, 50 degrees Fahrenheit

CHARACTERS

CPL. DAVE VAN DOMMELEN, Intelligence Division
CPL. TOM COMMISKEY, Assistant to CO
PVT. STEVE GAMMER, Lowly Company Runner

Subject: The Woes

TOM: I'm so damn funked.
DAVE: You mean fucked.
TOM: No, I mean funked.
DAVE: C'mon, Tom, be more specific.
TOM: Funked . . . down, I'm way down . . . funking down,
this operation stinks . . . And both you guys know it!
DAVE: Tom, why are you always so damned reluctant to
use the word fuck! It says so much more . . . Things are
so bad in this mission that everyone thinks—fuck no—
knows, we're in deep doo. Everyone's going around saying fuck! Why the fuck don't you!?

TOM: Well, maybe you're right but I *feel* funked out, just plain funked out in this goddamn stinking place.

STEVE: Oh for Christ's sake, Tom, will you shut the fuck up!

DAVE: See, Tom, you can funk up or down in this Army, but in Thule you can only fuck up.

TOM: Okay, okay, I know the difference! Now will the both of you do me a favor by shutting the fuck up!

6

Pillow Home

Whistling in the Light

Time, that most elusive of human inventions, became unfathomable.

Trying to take it all in barely one day after arriving, the crystal, stinging air both fascinated and repelled. Infinite images pushed and punished imaginations. Craggy icebergs and stark geologic formations, strange silences and stereoscopic sounds—a vast sky fleeced with clouds twisting and surging into weird designs—this initial experience spread reality into unknowable contortions.

It's not that we didn't try to make time a partial ally. Arriving when night was relinquishing its hold and day pushing into its own, we tried to harness time itself. Then night-day gradually narrowed and evaporated as the sun came to a complete halt as if fixed by superglue.

Circadian rhythms quickly went awry. No sunups and no sundowns inexorably skewed inner clocks. Early into the operation, to ensure a modicum of sleep, we installed heavy materials over the square double-paned windows—among them top secret maps—hopefully to cover up the cracks of rays sneaking through—which happened in any case. Guys staggered in and out of the sunlight at all hours, invariably cackling and cursing.

When the sun finally came to a total halt—or so it seemed to us—a baseball tournament got underway, the games commencing at precisely 12:01 a.m. Nearsighted as I was, the ball was a crystalline jewel and the hilarious running slightly opaque, unless the whiteouts or the burly winds or the floating snow brought about a midnight of silence.

41

The constant light never ceased to dazzle, illuminating odd hues and discordant shapes, conjuring up dreamy and scary thoughts. The constant light was both friend and enemy that forced the eyes onto the surrounding terrain in an endless going-around and coming-around.

Brownish fields eased into the dark green Thule harbor that was always filled with lazy, bobbing, blue-speckled icebergs, both tiny and massive. What appeared to be infertile tundra soil then totally surprised. Once the sun had begun to smile, the invincible permafrost softened into mush and lo, miniature life, freed from its frozen darkness, surged upward. Sprigs of willow brush flowers, green lichen, even tiny fir trees, speckled the small fields and hills.

A fixed lightbulb, the sun's insistent glare bounced off the snow-covered hills, the looming glaciers, and the icy fjord, forcing unwanted tears. But on a moment's notice, it could surrender to a whiteout.

Whiteouts: mention of the very word itself terrorized us all. A mixture of exceedingly fine white snow fused with thick fog, whiteouts were gauze over the eyes that lasted for minutes or hours. They obliterated corporeality. Furiously blinking, eyes stared in disbelief as one's arms and legs, the hills and buildings, the blue sky, everything, all suddenly disappeared. Whiteouts evoked mirthful scenes as well, like those limbs that hovered several feet above the ground in which case the only sight was scurrying feet scooting along the roads.

But when the base siren harshly announced the arrival of a whiteout, to prevent chaos and demise, everybody made a beeline for the nearest shelter. Planes circled, then were ordered into a holding pattern, waiting, praying for the whiteout to lift, and finally, desperately, heading south to another airbase in central Greenland before the fuel gave out.

Yet it was bound to happen, and a little more than a decade after TRARG had departed, a B-52 bomber laden with four hydrogen bombs lost its bearing in a whiteout and crashed into the surrounding seabed. The State Department notified Denmark, positively assuring its officials that the plane had been located and its bombs retrieved. Protocol coupled with fear had surely dictated such a positive assurance because in fact one bomb had actually remained elusive and has never been found.

To our relief, the constant, biting winds gradually moderated, though they never gave up winter's insistence. On occasion they roared in when least expected. The air's crispness became downright invigorating and it never got hot. When the winds did abate, guys tore off shirts to bask in the summer warmth. According to the weather people, who monitored every quantity every hour on the hour, the average temperatures were –4 in April, 21 in May, 36 in June, 41 in July, 39 in August, and 28 in September (Fahrenheit).

So jolting were the incongruities that everyone desperately wanted to record mind-boggling scenarios. Cameras went anywhere, everywhere. Alcohol and poker had its addicts, but picture-snapping gripped everyone. Those who didn't have cameras made an immediate run to the PX, and those who did, upgraded. Over the months thousands of pictures were snapped detailing every nook and cranny, then laboriously mounted between slides, and endlessly reviewed in countless projector shows. Thule had become a tableau of singular experiences that somehow added up to a collective consciousness expressed in zeeewooows, if ever such a word exists to express a Jungian image.

6. Tent City surrounded by permafrost.

Top-Secret Gypsies

"Men," rasped the six-striped sergeant smugly at the opening day of basic training, "don't ever forget: Home is where your pillow is at!" That line is a bona fide classic. It has rung in my mind with every move during and after my military stint.

A month into operations at the air force's brand new, shiny, aluminum quarters, TRARG was ordered out to another location. Who the hell knew why? The C.O. knew, and he was plenty ripshit, but that didn't change a thing. Nor did the officers say why, least of all to the historian. Apparently the air force hierarchy just didn't like their turf being taken over by a bunch of creepy top-secret army troops whose mission might undercut their prestige.

Turf conveys status, and TRARG was shifted to a locale that reflected the bottom of the dung-heap. TRARG wound up at the edge of the base adjacent to the massive garbage dump.

Huge waste deposits abutting the perimeter of the bay were an eyesore, albeit at times a whimsical mélange. Since the impervious tundra made it impossible to bury even a toothpick and environmental issues meant nothing at the time, what couldn't be burned or dumped into the fjord spread out along the coast and went hilly up. Debris from all over the metropolis kept coming, and coming, day in season out. Each day the cragged, uneven garbage stretched wider and higher, rivaling the one natural small mountain in the region, Mount Dundas, which stood proudly guarding the harbor.

Piles of pyramidal mounds offered an industrial tribute to Dadaism.

Waiting gulls, polar bears, and seals eagerly devoured tons of discarded food. The myriad discards also attracted Outak and his Inuit villagers, who scoured its innards, upgrading their hunting weapons and complementing their furniture in sparse quarters. At the same time, they were deeply troubled by its adverse affects. Later, in a dramatic action, the villagers turned their backs on American trash and presence. Suddenly, which is to say unannounced, they simply upped and left, disappearing into the vast terrain of northern Greenland.

Within a week, there emerged our tiny TRARG compound, a minis-cule complex of tents and Atwells (a cylindrical building) consisting of a rudimentary mess hall, medical facility, storage bins, wooden outhouses, and an assortment of other work buildings. Short rocky streets skirting in and out ended in a cul-de-sac. Large discarded oil drums filled with rocks anchored tents and Atwells against the ferocious winds that blew in, even during the unruffled summer months.

A gooey tundra quagmire encircled the whole camp. More than one yelping guy was pried out after a hard bout of drinking.

Precious weeks of daylight were totally lost in this relocating process. Meanwhile, work crews proceeded to build a Nuna Takeoff Camp and other smaller bases at the edge of the ice cap, in order to conduct equip-ment experiments, and proceed onto the ice cap.

Obstacles wreaked havoc with the tight schedule. The lack of parts, equipment failures, adverse weather conditions, human errors, all multi-plied on a daily basis. TRARG was falling behind in its experiments and its projected endgame.

TRARG Hippies

We pencil pushers moved into a large domed structure. Spacey and comfy, we set up our operations and whizzed into high gear. Perhaps the pillows were finally in the right place.

Distance from the center of Thule, however, made a crucial difference. As our work extended around the clock into endless weeks, all protocol was discarded. Contrary to regulations, mustaches sprouted and mish-mash fatigues sidled into arctic gear. By a few scant years, in cool dress and antimilitary style, we had preceded the hippies of Haight-Ashbury.

Wherever we went in "downtown" Thule, so designated even though it was barely half a mile or so down the dirt roads, the air force boys glared at us. It wasn't too long before the skirmishes began. One day my main buddy, the mild-mannered Dave, wanted some books, so off we went to the Thule base library. It was closed, no excuse offered on the front door, so instead we trekked over to the plush noncommissioned officers club.

We had just begun trying our hands at the dartboard when a guy with stripes came over. Nastily scrutinizing us from the shoes up, he rendered a sharp judgment: "All right you guys, it's against regulations to play games in fatigues . . . if those are fatigues! . . . What the fuck do you guys have on anyway!?"

"Hey," Dave explained, "we're not air force and this is our uniform. We're TRARG, the outfit near the dump. This is standard operating procedure for us."

"Fuckoff, pronto," he snapped, "or I'll haul your asses in."

"Now isn't that the height of stupidity," Dave wrote home to his wife, Mike, that evening, "Here we are—thousands of miles from where anyone can see you—they make regulations like that. We were really pissed off."

"Shades of *Willie and Joe*," Dave wrote; it was as if nothing had happened since World War II when cartoonist Bill Mauldin depicted an identical scenario for Willie and Joe, the frontline GIs in the Italian campaign who had been sloughing from one foxhole to another. In a short rest and relaxation center far behind the front lines, they were harassed for violating . . . a dress code.

Then the air force lowered the gauntlet. Although only thirty of us noncoms had been eating in their main mess hall, TRARG was ordered nevertheless to perform KP and guard duties. So there we were, top specialists atop the world on a top-secret operation, reduced to nonrated flunkies. Naturally, it was the draftees who were sentenced since anyone above sergeant was exempt, and all of us were beneath that rank.

It was time to get the hell out of Thule! Everyone applied to go to Nuna Takeoff at the edge of the ice cap, then under construction for the great crevasse-crossing experiments. Gleeful at getting away from the inane regulations and into the gritty aspect of the mission, some managed to make it over. Not all, though, and not me. "Not you self-adorned pencil pushers," declared the C.O., "I need you here for intelligence and historical reporting and other paper work. For now you men will stick around!"

We wound up arms deep cleaning air force cooking vats. Making the weekly deadline for the status reports became impossible.

Screw history, Pentagon!

7. Waiting for the bus to Brooklyn.

(Sub)Enemies

Perverse forces, hardships mounting over the many months, cumulated to suckle all.

Military life is a nomadic grind under any circumstance but a potpourri of quirky ingredients brewed and stewed in Thule's tundra pot. Numerous everythings, subenemies in effect, had a hand stirring the cauldron: remoteness from wives and lovers and children; Moscow radio tracking our movements; hidden and silent crevasses serenely white; reality-obliterating whiteouts; "Dear John" letters; "invisible" thermonuclear bombers slipping in and out; unspoken feelings; and time miming time all the time.

Flitting around the camp, invoking a whimsical ditty, the pencil pusher and statistical boggling sports authority Bernie Reiner lent his voice to the solidarity of separateness:

Let us worry not unduly,
Nor dread the time you spend in Thule.
Be contented as you should,
You've never had it quite so good!

Deep within, though, were palpable differences. It mattered whether you were a regular or draftee, from one geographical region or another, went to college or not, bathed regularly or rarely. TRARG consisted mainly of Southern and Midwestern Baptists and Methodists, a smattering of Northeastern Catholics, and seven Jews—or was it six? Being married or single, a stickler-on-regulations or not-giving-a-shit, a hard worker or a piss-off, an adroit storyteller or lousy listener, a snotty poker winner or snide loser: on such minor matters did relationships tangle, criss-cross, link.

Since it was my job to secure progress reports from every division, sooner or later I got to know many in the outfit. Working against a strict deadline, I found myself constantly pleading, cajoling, and haranguing for the summaries to come in on time. This problem propelled me into unnatural graciousness, not an easy task because a simmering anger had constantly fueled my temperament since early childhood.

Dave, I learned later from a letter to Mike, misinterpreted this behavior, though there was some validity in his assessment: "He's a little vain and domineering," he wrote, "but on the whole he is very easy to get along with. He likes to be well known and makes the effort of introducing himself to everyone new in the outfit—especially if he thinks that their position is good enough."

Dave was an artist—his forte would become fiber art—whose father labored at the General Motors plant in Flint, Michigan. I was instantly elated upon meeting him. An artisan! Had the army bureaucrats truly recognized the importance of aestheticism? Was Dave selected to record this top-secret mission in inks, watercolors, maybe oils? A new type of draftee, a canvas soldier!?

No freaking way! The army had put him in charge of the outfit's intelligence security apparatus. Though low in the military chain-of-being, it fell upon Dave to certify every person, map, report, and memo, and it was his luck of the draw that he had to report to the acknowledged worst officer in TRARG, Captain Phillip Lament.

Lament was the sole officer who drew his inspiration from the depths of the anal. Strict, overbearing, arrogant, and stocked with grandiosity, his unalloyed impulse was to intrude himself into every aspect of the operation. And, as they say, these were his good qualities. His worst included a tendency toward sloppiness. This left Dave to clean up after him. So the intricate pathways of intelligence of this secret operation were largely in the hands of an artist.

Slightly framed, his reddish hair tousled about under his cap, Dave possessed remarkable eyes. They seemed to focus everywhere all at once. It was his way of overseeing life from an unusual perspective. Not only did he run the entire intelligence apparatus, constantly wrestling with the military's arcane regulations and tussling with the insufferable Captain Lament, he offered help to anyone who was behind the eight-ball. His upbeat bounce was the antidote to the heavy anger that too often hobbled my own energies.

Dave and I became co-conspirators, skirting regulations, compiling a secret file, and flitting in and around the tundra canvassing icebergs. At night, we plunged into politics and literature and mused about everything, especially the identity of the Pentagon plant in the outfit. Who-in-hell-was-he??

It was not unusual for high-level missions to be covertly monitored by an agent from the Counter Intelligence Corps, someone in a key position who wires directly to the Pentagon.

8. Pencil Pushers' Palace.

Dave Goes Red

A month after our first relocation, our pillows were shifted again!

Captain Phillip Lament wanted our posh Atwell for his headquarters and for his personal living quarters. Dave and I fought him on and off for weeks, a battle we knew was lost but his power-grabbing pissed us off.

He won, and off we went to other quarters.

A tent! A fucking ten-man tent in northern Greenland!! Picking up our gear and pillows, six of us pencil pushers piled in. Regulars and draftees together under a rickety canvas roof. The regulars, like Sergeants Lee Cupps and Dave Sexton, hailing from south of the Mason-Dixon line, managed key units. Politically conservative yet soft on spit-and-polish, they knew their stuff and rarely pulled rank on us—unless the C.O. passed along an order for the entire company whereupon they would stand erect in the middle of the tent and throatily intone, "Men, y'all hear, it's time to side up."

Tom and Steve, the two other draftees whose genetic strands were at opposite species ends, were the odd couple before Neil Simon had ever conceived of such a mix. A strict Catholic who looked and acted like a novitiate, Tom elevated the meaning of prim and proper. A stickler for efficiency and order, these skills attracted the C.O. who elevated him as his personal secretary. On occasion, though, he totally flip-flopped and allowed a looser side to take over.

Steve, on the other hand, was the sole remaining private in the outfit, demoted to courier because of his maverick, cool, and unkempt ways. Just the year before he had been catching passes as a tight end on the Michigan State University footfall team. Several eccentric hobbies catapulted him into singularity. Even before his eyes had focused on early morning rising, he sloppily guzzled down a beer and recited passages from his favorite author, Shakespeare. Steve was the outfit's outstanding enigma.

Once settled into Arctic tenting, we hoisted up glasses to our latest abode. Dave painted a sign to front the tent with the logo "The Three Ps," short for Pencil Pushers' Palace. Inside our olive-green enclosure were several squat oil stoves with metal pipes soaring twelve feet through the roof, a bunch of roving chairs and footlockers, and top-secret materials mixed with magazines and books scattered in all directions. The canvas smelled of a thousand camphor balls vintage Second World War. Or, maybe we joked, the First.

At the far end were my bed, a small desk, and typewriter. Jammed into this space was the Historical Division. A tiny library came into existence when a batch of paperback books sent from some Washington office wound up at my desk. More books mysteriously arrived at intervals. Dave and I set up a lending post and never again set foot in the air force library.

Buddy Dave, though, was not a happy camper. He went around muttering about the dreary surroundings. Using a literary approach I tried to assuage him: "Dave, this is fucking Greenland. This is godforsaken Thule. This is stupid-ass TRARG. It may seem like eternity but it's only for a short while. What difference does it make?!"

His mutterings only got longer and louder. Stupidly, I tried a nonsensical tact: "Okay, Dave, this is fucking war, not with the Russians but with the ice cap, maybe even the air force. It's supposed to look like hell. War is hell—isn't this what the man once said. And this is cold hell. Get used to it!"

His gentle blue eyes wondered deep into me, a cross between sympathy and curiosity. Saying not another word, Dave's wild artistry flew into action. On a small sign attached to a tent pole, he announced that he was going to coat the barrels encircling the tent that held it down from taking off in the wild blue yonder "an ungodly red." Then he disappeared.

Scouring the labyrinths of the base he managed to purloin buckets of paint from a civilian work crew and two days later the metal barrels, plus the rocks surrounding the tent, glistened in the midnight sun. Surveying the results from the tundra street—a dark-green tent with two black metal witch-hat spheres protruding from its roof totally interred in bright crimson barrels and rocks—Dave proudly exclaimed, "This place looks like a misplaced carnival!" A week later Moscow Molly and Leningrad Lenny tersely announced that its MIGs had spotted an American insult: the imperialists at Thule had mocked its Revolutionary symbol! Dave's glistening red artistry had inadvertently increased Cold War tensions. He deserves a footnote in the history of warfare.

Tundra Souls

The PPP became the center of social swirls. Draftees, and some regulars, constantly swooped in, trading stories, playing games, cranking up the slide projector, and tossing epithets around about the mission. Geologists flitted in and out with their misshapen rocks and rundown of geologic time and crevasses, constantly challenging anyone to a game of Battleship and always winning. Poker games sprang up at a moment's notice; supply guys brazenly bartered deals. Drinking consumption reached new highs until the booze ran out, and then scouting parties went to bargain with the fly boys.

All the while, the good Sergeants Cupps and Sexton kept the radio dial tuned to their hillbilly music, a grating, awful sound to us Northeasterners.

There were no problems of privacy because none existed. Exhaustion from the nonstop workweek initially left everyone impotent though gradually sexual frustrations overwhelmed. When masturbation occurred, the wind muffled out sounds. Tears shed came and went with the winds; virtually everyone at one time or another cried over some problem thousands of miles away in some remote other world as the isolation gradually wore everyone down.

Dave and Tom decided to do something about morale. A newsletter, *The Midnight Sun*, its logo crafted by Dave, became a weekly sortie. It contained a hodgepodge of items, international and national events, sports, birthdays, promotions, classifieds, and inspiration from the Chaplain. Juxtapositions were inadvertent, so Dave and Tom claimed:

6 June 1953

Partly Cloudy, High 32 above
CHAPLIN'S CORNER
God's Minutes

Someone has said that in an average life of 70 years time would be used somewhat as follows: 8 years in amusements; six years at the dinner table; 5 years in transportation; 4 for conversation; 14 years in work; 3 years in reading; 24 years in sleeping; and 3 years in convalescence. But how much time does a man give God? If he went to religious services every day for five minutes and to church every Sunday for 45 minutes and prayed for five minutes every evening, he would be giving five months to God—five months out of seventy-five years.

✳ ★ ✳

CLASSIFIEDS
WANTED: One woman. Contact any male at TRARG.

"Crevasse" Ron, an enterprising engineer, howled at the Chaplain's math. The figures, he pointed out, didn't exactly tabulate. But what the hell, he gave the Chaplain credit for a spiritual reach under such unusual circumstances.

God Bless All French Scientists

Boredom was never a problem as one logistical obstacle after another upset schedules, driving the company crazy trying to accomplish its primary tasks within the severe time constraints. Shortages of materials, equipment breakdowns coupled with a paucity of spare parts, climatic consternation, and jealous wrangling complicated matters. Even shortages of bodies betided; the company was woefully undermanned. All this produced organizational bleeding, the shifting of personnel from one task to a contrary one, resulting in more frustration and weariness.

Too much frustration and too little frolic took its toll and guys grew grumpy and grumpier, lashing out at the brass for what was presumed their oafishness and inefficiency. Breaks from the weeks in and weeks out pace were a rare commodity. So guys took off into the surrounding hills and hid out for hours. Or disappeared into "downtown Thule" to any one of a spate of mammoth air force buildings.

Every now and then a USO show came through Thule, but as time was tight, we took little notice. Once, though, word came down that a USO troupe would actually perform at the remote Nuna Takeoff Camp at the edge of the ice cap! Everyone instantly perked up: hey, did you hear, real women, WOMEN!! Takeoff Camp was pint-sized, and it was clear that the USO troopers would be forced to perform in the tiny mess hall. This meant cramming, which was just fine with the guys because it would have offered a chance to socialize with females for the first time in months. Then the brass snafued the situation: the men were to be kept at a distance. Preparing for the USO's arrival, the stupid-ass major promptly declared that he would "courts-martial anyone even talking to a woman." Even talking?!

Anxious over downward morale, the C.O. ordered a 16-mm film projector. Flicks! Not exactly first-run films but who the hell cared! The first movie was the six-year-old *The Jolson Story* (1946), starring Larry Parks. No one in the outfit paid any attention to the blackface stereotyping, a common popular culture motif. And no one, I thought, was paying any attention to the plot, the conflict between an immigrant Cantor father and his entertainer son pursuing the American Dream, the pair finally reconciling in a touching scene of a Yom Kippur service during the holiest of Jewish holidays.

But it was weird watching this ethnic conflict in Northern Greenland with the ice cap looming as a backdrop. When the mess hall lights went on, a sergeant from the hills of Arkansas tapped me on the shoulder. "Hey Joe," he said in a warm, ingratiating tone, "I had matzey ball soup once. Hey, fuckin' good. You Jews have real good food." He was the same sergeant who, during our negotiation about his Leica camera, said easily, "Hey, Joe, you tryin' to Jew me down!?" "Dale," I replied, "are you tryin' to Christian me up!?" He didn't get it at first and kept peering at me quizzically. Then we both cracked up.

If the film was a droplet quencher, the second one was an exploding firecracker. After learning that there were no "wimmon" at Thule, the French scientists instantly wired their Parisian friends for a porno flick. That night the war with the enemies could have begun and no one would have noticed. When word spread that an X-rated film was in the offing, every project near and beyond the ice cap was abandoned. The major who had put the verboten boundary on the USO females was smart enough to let this one alone. So crowded was the small mess hall that guys almost sat on one another's laps. Not a soul complained that the film was in French. Somehow subtitles weren't required. The nonstop yelping echoed off the ice cap, probably triggering off a couple of icebergs into the fjord.

Instant heroes, the French scientists were besieged for more. Then the projector broke, and there were no parts to fix it.

7

Midnight Requisitions in the Land of the Midnight Sun

Discon–tented

No matter the locale, everyone posed the same nauseating question: where the fuck is reality at . . . ?

In early April, when we had deplaned at Thule, it was half-dusk/half-light. At reveille the next morning, after a short, lousy sleep, the screw-loose Captain Page lined us up and ordered us to "police the area." In military lingo, this is the practice of fanning out and picking up debris, such as cigarette butts.

But this was the Arctic and of course there was nothing on the ground save tundra rocks. The order had nothing to with sanitizing the area; it had everything to do with maintaining discipline. We all stared at him. "Stupid ass," someone loudly whispered. "Hey, Joe, isn't this the first top-secret policing in the history of the world?!" We piled up all the rocks we could scoop.

By the time we moved into our so-called permanent camp a month later, any thought of protocol had vanished from the spit-and-polish mentality. That's because the mission was in deep trouble, far behind from the very moment of its conception, and its execution was proving onerous. Results were all that mattered. Dave wrote to his wife Mike, "This madhouse gets worse and worse. I just cannot believe that this outfit is capable of staying together for more than a day."

Everything went awry. Communication between headquarters and the outlying Nuna Takeoff Camp was often hampered by weather;

helicopters broke down and repair parts were scarce; sonar equipment seeking hidden crevasses failed to locate them; top-secret materials were misplaced or simply disappeared; whiteouts and wind storms shut down movement for days at a time.

Still, amazingly, ongoing experiments went forth. When technology failed, ingenuity prevailed. Perhaps the most creative was to tether the six-foot-six electrical engineer draftee Ron to a long nylon rope attached to a weasel, a tracked vehicle. A long pole in one hand, Ron slowly jammed it into the deep snow seeking hidden crevasses, and at times half-plunged up to his waist when locating them.

If all this were not enough, the outfit had to contend with the dozens of VIPs from the Pentagon, Congress, and Western European countries who were intrigued by TRARG's scientific and military experiments. Many of them, though, were just sight-seekers, intrigued with the exotic idea of being up in the high Arctic and flirting with the North Pole. Fussed at, wined and dined, helicoptered from one camp to another, the VIPs disrupted schedules and depleted dwindling supplies. They also carried the latest cameras, snapping pictures of anything that moved, particularly the tracked weasel Snow-Cats. Especially high on their list were the massive icebergs. And who could blame them?

Hardly a one posed questions to any of the specialist-draftees, however, or the historian, understandably so since they had been purposely steered away by the C.O. They returned to Washington, London, Paris, or wherever, their reports glowing with technological findings and accomplishments.

This led to the second major conflict between the C.O. and me.

Ripshit

Elder Sergeant Sexton came into our tent and I could tell he was steaming. He pointed his finger right at my head. "Joe, what in hell did you write in your latest report?"

I stopped typing. "Sex," I tried joshing to offset his occasional notorious anger, "nothing, nothing, *really*."

That didn't mollify him one bit. Normally, his southern gentility softened disturbing situations. "Fuck off, Joe, I just came from C.O.'s office.

I no sooner stopped to tell him somethin' or other when he dressed me down for doin' somethin' stupid—but then he said it was nothin' compared to y'all's greater stupidity."

When I made the mistake of asking him "what??" his face got red and he really let loose. "The C.O. is holl-eerin' blue shit, tellin' everyone in sight what an asshole you are for writin' about the bigwigs comin' here and disruptin' schedules and usin' up valuable space in the helicopters and all kinds of shit like that. Did y'all really put that in the report and expect the C.O. to sign on before it went sailin' off to the Pentagon!?"

He stopped momentarily, regaining his breath. "Even Tom, poor Tom," he tried to get back to some sort of calm, "who came to your defense was cut down by the C.O. A few more stupid-ass things like that and y'all have no one in this company who'll even speak to you—and then who knows, y'all be accidentally left out on the cap for some hungry polar bear. Get it!!"

I threw up my hands. "Goddammit, what am I supposed to do, whitewash the situation? You know as well as I do that these damned weekend warriors are creating havoc with the place!"

"Yeah," Sexton shot back, "no fuckin' doubt about it! So what! After the C.O. somewhat calmed down, he told me to tell you that history matters but PR matters more. Do you know what PR stands for, asshole!?"

"Oh for Pete's sake, Sexton, I know, I know—the C.O. and I have had this quarrel before. He's heavy on the public relations side of things."

Sexton smiled in that silly, dangerous Southern grin. "Joe, the 'P' in that phrase is now synonymous for Pentagon. And the C.O. told me to really size it up for you. So, here goes: PENTAGON . . . Now y'all got it!?"

I nodded, and went back to my typing. This time I was scared.

Always Know Your Real Enemy . . .

The urgency for basic equipment and spare parts became a major priority. There was no time to wait for anything to come from the States. Summer would be over in an Arctic wink. Requesting materials from the air force that was motivated either by indifference or envy, or both, was also out of the question. The situation clearly called for imaginative tactics. It was time, in short, for "midnight requisitions," this artful phrase referring to acceptable pilfering from any branch of the military, provided one didn't get caught.

Thule was ripe for second-story jobs but in this case it wasn't necessary to go that high since most of the buildings were ranch-style level. At the same time, base construction was still ongoing. The air force would never know what hit them.

It all came to a head one night when a group of us were sitting around the tent devouring a batch of Mess Sergeant Gadget's really scrumptious cookies and washing them down with first-rate bourbon someone had scrounged from the C.O.'s special cache. Sexton and Cupps were lying around reading magazines and humming along to hillbilly music. Tom tried to shut it out by working away on the next issue of the *Midnight Sun*.

Several geologists, Gil and Don, had come by after an excursion identifying rock strata from a remote valley and were polishing off a round of Battleship. Botanist Herb was resting up after indexing miniature flowers that had suddenly popped up in the adjacent fields. Statistician Bernie had strolled in from scheduling his midnight volleyball tournament. Engineer Ron, still breathing, had just pulled in from scouting for crevasses.

It didn't take long for the bitching to begin. Everyone had his favorite complaint but apart from mauling the brass the lament was about the shortage of things. What made it worse was that the air force was laden down with surpluses. "Them sonsofbitches," said Gil dryly, pointing upbase, "they've everything up the kazoo, and in spades. What's more, they won't loan a thing, can you believe not even for a day!"

Ron chimed in, evincing an innocence that belied most of us draftees, "I tried to get a voltage meter and they told me to fuck off, or something equally creative like that."

Bernie was also furious. All he wanted was a couple of volleyballs for the midnight games, and they told him to fuck off as well.

"We're running out of typewriter ribbons," I groused. "Nothing doing when I rung up one of the nicer guys I met at the command office. He didn't tell me to fuck off but he did say that if he asked his supply sergeant he would definitely tell him to tell me to get fucking lost."

And so it went, "everyone tryin' to get into the act," as the great comedian Jimmy Durante would have put it.

The subject was about spent when Sexton opened up. More often than not when we draftees held session he held off wise-cracks save a smattering of snorts. On this day, for no apparent reason, he was in a foul mood. He sat up in his bunk and cut loose in a raspy voice. "Bitch! All you fuckin' draftees do is bitch! You guys been in for almost a year now, and y'all still haven't got a fuckin' clue how the system works. Y'all want somethin,' get the fuck OUT and get IT." He glared for a moment, then swung back onto his pillow, and ripped open his magazine.

We wanted to laugh but held back. Not a good idea to get Sexton madder. His buddy in the next bunk, the gentle Cupps, also got into the act. "A-MEN," was about all he said but it was intoned with good-old Southern boy lilt.

Like most of the regulars, Sexton and Cupps gave us a lot of room yet also resented our college pedigrees. At one time or another along the way in the grueling days and months, the regulars would point out how stupid we were about things military: "You guys' fuckin' degrees don't mean shit in combat."

"We hear you loud and clear, Sergeants," said Ron, baldly deferential. "Okay, just how do we get what we need?"

Sexton was not about to get any more involved. He lowered his magazine, rolled his eyes over at Cupps and with a sigh of exasperation said cryptically, "Midnight Requisitions, assholes!"

Sexton was right on target. In addition to supplies, we were badly in need of some risky diversion.

Dave's artistic mind was already at work. "I guess the thing to do is to draw up a list of things we need immediately, then figure out how to get 'em." With what seemed like a single motion, the scientists pulled out their pens and furiously jotted away. Around the tent went a master sheet. No one asked for anything personal, though there were guffaws when we agreed that a better quality toilet paper should be the highest requirement!

The list was the easy part. When the items were categorized, the difficulties became apparent: scientific equipment alongside sporting goods alongside office supplies alongside toilet paper, items scattered in different buildings around Thule. There would have to be a series of these raids, an impossible task under the best of circumstances. How could we even come close to achieving half the list when there was no darkness? Can't exactly slink around unnoticed on a Midnight Requisition with the sun beaming down at midnight.

"Brazen it out, that's how," Herb said emphatically, and then added, "but I don't know exactly what the hell it means!?"

"Well, thanks," said Gil, slightly sarcastic. "Yep, botanists are only good when it comes to what's obviously in the ground."

Doubting Tom No More

"Well, I know what Ron means, even if he doesn't."

All eyes turned to Tom, who normally kept his counsel unless someone cursed too much—then his strict religious upbringing reared up and he tried to silence the offending individual. "Please," he would say quietly, forcibly, "that's overextending."

Of all us draftees, Tom took regulations literally, constantly invoking the "good book," meaning the army manuals. "By the book," he would intone, "we would have to do it by the book!"

A neatnik, Tom was also the only one in the tent who kept his clothes in proper shape, his shoes polished, and his bed trim. Personally he was a poster boy for any monkish order: no hanging fatigues, no mustache, no unruly hair. He set a terrible standard for the slovenly rest of us, even including the sergeants. Despite all this, we held Tom in great affection because of his selflessness and unthreatening demeanor. He spoke in a singsong tone, as if his choir experience had never left him.

So it came as a shock when he exclaimed, "What I think we have to do is go on scavenger hunts."

"Scavenger hunts??" asked Herb, and then quickly answered his question, "Oh, you mean the garbage dump. I was just down there yesterday and spotted a new batch of mini-flowers."

"Yeah," said Tom, "beaucoup stuff, much of it in good shape or near enough so we could repair it. We could send out raiding parties!"

"Raiding parties, Tom, you're too much," I chimed in. "You, who live by the book and accuse us of straying across lines, you want us to raid the dumps? You know they're off-limits. This is serious stuff."

The air force police had checkpoints at various stops around the huge heap. Identification was needed to get into the place. Special forms would also be required. Uniforms would have to be air force. Then there was the problem of vehicles. Since some of our trucks were on loan from the air force, this might be a partial solution but an empty truck going in was sure to create suspicion. Besides, who among us could handle the big trucks? We were mere college draftees.

I thought fast, trying to come up with something just to save face. "Okay, I'll tell you one thing that would work. First we get official stationery, which Tom can do because he has access to the C.O.'s desk—right?" Out of the corner of my eye I thought I saw Tom blanch. "And fake letters with the C.O.'s signature. On occasion he asks for the loan of a jeep or a truck. Hell, we could have a letter asking for damaged stuff, or anything we want down there—mainly smaller items, though, anything else real big would be tricky."

"Hold on a minute!" Tom was flushed. "You want *me* to steal official stationery from the Colonel's desk? No way. *No!*"

Poor Tom. Everyone burst out laughing, not at him because we all knew his boundaries, it's just that he sounded so distraught, so caught in his own offering. And I was on a roll. "Listen Tom, there's no way he would ever notice any loss of stationery. His signature? Okay, that's a problem. Who here is a good forger?" No one spoke up.

That seemed to end the Great-Draftee-Caper before it even began.

Tom broke the silence. Speaking in a subdued voice, he slowly raised both his hands, "I think it can be done with perfect legitimacy. By the book, I mean, at least the C.O.'s letter . . ."

"Tom, spell it out, carefully," said Dave.

"Look, the C.O. has made previous requests for stuff. I can easily ask for a letter of authorization to scour the dump for certain things. He'll approve of that, I'm sure."

Everyone agreed that that was the way to go. Then Sexton put down his magazine. Keeping his eyes glued to the tent's ceiling, he softly drawled, "Yeah, sounds good, ah like it. My boy Cupps likes it, too, right Cuppy?" Cupps nodded. "But a good midnight requisition needs a combination of items to make it foolproof. All you got now is the openin' wedge. Y'all got to go one step further."

"What step?" asked Don, thinking like the smart geologist he was. "What do we need more than the Colonel's letter?"

Sexton kept talking, his voice and eyes straight up to the top of the tent. "Because y'all are missing things here, somethin' only us pros would understan'. Y'see, the guards gonna look into the truck and see only privates and maybe a corporal. No sergeants, no officers, and y'all with only one stripe. No fuckin' way he's not gonna get suspicious."

"Well, in that case," exclaimed Don, throwing down a gauntlet, "why don't you or Cupps come with us?"

Cupps cackled. "No way, college boys, no fuckin' way. You're on your own but Sexton and me'll help you pull it off. Only one thing, our names, mums all the way—you hear us!"

A chorus of nodding draftees tried to assure them.

Swinging up from his prone position, Sexton looked straight at us. "Okay, here's the way to go. First, y'all get with Rich in Supply. Even though he's like y'all, a lowly draftee, he's one of the best dealers in the outfit. Fact is, he's got the balls of us regulars—so get 'im to trade somethin' for an air force uniform with sergeant stripes. Then ol' boy Steve with his football shoulders dons the uniform when y'all go to the dump. Yup, that'll do it!" Cupps let out a supporting "whoopee."

This was going a bit too far. It was one thing to con the C.O., another to impersonate an air force sergeant. Sexton had singled out Steve because he didn't give a hoot about anything military, but as usual he was nowhere to be seen. "Yeah, Steve's just right for it but where the hell has he been these past couple of days?" someone asked.

"Then he's out," said Sexton harshly.

Who among us would be willing to pull off the caper? Not me, I thought, that's for sure. And none of us draftees in that tent would even come close to crossing *that* line.

How wrong I was.

Tom broke the silence, "I would love to do it."

I would swear the canvas tent moved a foot because of the booming laughter.

"Cut the bullshit, Tom," several piped up at once.

Tom's choir-boy face went beet red. "No, I mean it. I love acting. I've always wanted to be an actor. I didn't major in it at Boston College but I swear I was in a lot of plays. I'm telling you," he said pleadingly, "I could pull it off!"

Dave and I exchanged skeptical thoughts after the plans were finalized. "Go figure," said Dave with a chuckle, "here's Tom who recoils at the idea of stealing stationery from the C.O., refuses to use cusswords, insists on doing things 'by the book', and now he wants to perform, can you believe it, in a way-out, illegal, operation by impersonating an air force sergeant!"

I didn't know it at the time, but Tom had taught me a valuable lesson in the convoluted pathways of contradictions.

Supply hustler PFC Rich was only too delighted to be part of the action, provided that he got part of the action, he said. In short time, he had the uniform and in equally short time, the great air force rip-off got underway with the eagerness of college freshmen at a beer party.

We stole them blind!

Steve, though, who had so coveted the title of iconoclast, the army shafter, was miffed that Tom had one-upped him.

A-Tenting We Will Go

Practicing Russian

Rumor in our outfit was that in the upcoming war, the USSR forces would opt to capture Thule Air Base intact rather than obliterate it. The consensus was that, no fools they, the Russians would overwhelm the base via a massive paratrooper attack. Once in control, they would use it as a launching pad for bombing North American targets. Just how valid this analysis was no one really knew for sure, but all my buddies were in agreement on this one. In these tight quarters we also occasionally overheard the brass discussing this strategy from the same vantage point.

Confirmation further came from headquarter instructions for Thule's defense. At the sound of the siren signaling an attack, every man was to grab a carbine, or whatever, thus fully prepared to engage the troops descending from the sky.

Consequently on those rare occasions when the alarm beckoned, our small albeit valiant TRARG performed as model soldiers, especially the regulars, many of whom had combat experience during the Second World War.

At the very first alert, as per instructions, we dashed to the supply tent to get our carbine rifles. Rich was there, smiling his broker smile but with palms up. Somehow, somewhere, in our frequent moves from one quarter to another, the carbines had been misplaced and were nowhere to be located. Or so Rich had contended. A truly sweet guy, but we suspected he had traded them away for something or other.

Right up front, though, was a full supply of shining protractors. Frustrated, still fairly dutiful, TRARG nonetheless grouped together in the semi-frozen permafrost fields looking anxiously up into the sky for the incoming onslaught.

On the horizon, Russian MIGs were barreling in, streaking toward the base but our fighter jets had already *sssshhuuusssed* from their individual catapults to intercept them. Empty-handed, we cheered our boys with "go get 'ims." In a few moments, upon naturally spotting our jets, there were the vanishing vapors of MIGs heading back to their Arctic base, and then an endless, cerulean sky.

Just a test of our mettle, and we proudly dispersed to return to our Cold War mission.

On the second call-to-carbines, Rich had somehow "miraculously" located our weapons. By early summer, our zeal remained but we overlooked something crucial, and it wasn't the Soviets. It was the permafrost! Over the many weeks, the relentless sun had melted down its top layer, and now it was all gooey.

Like a slow-motion film, we gradually sank into the muck, our legs going ankle-deep, and suddenly it was not possible to budge. The Soviets had us! When the last man finally extricated himself, there were rounds of highly creative cursing about the higher echelon: Brass Permafrosted Brains.

Discussing this dire scenario after the mishap, a number of us draftees decided to concede the base. We would lay down in the snowy muck and offer up our best Russian. To this end every so often we practiced our opening greeting in the worst Russian accent imaginable:

> Welcome to Thule Comrade Soldiers of the Glorious USSR. We hope you
> will be comfortable here. Stay with our blessings. Now please allow us
> to return to our wonderful families. Goodbye.

A more practical fervent hope was that the paratroopers would alight squarely in the tundra's permafrost. Becoming totally mired and rendered ineffective, they would then surrender without protest—or else suffer terribly from a counterattack from those of us hiding in the wooden-floored tents and Atwells armed with carbines and protractors.

No Purple Hearts!?

Notwithstanding the Soviet's sure-fire plan to overtake Thule, a more imminent threat bedeviled. A trifling matter was the tons of bodily waste that accumulates from thousands of men, the visiting Congress members, plus the single woman and her two children and dog. Where to dispose of such large quantities of natural substances? From the beginning of Thule's construction years before TRARG had arrived, this had been a monumental headache.

The impervious tundra terrain rendered outdoor plumbing piping impossible. So huge convoys of septic tank trucks carted the waste from the barracks to the shoreline and released it into the surrounding fjords. There can be little doubt that five thousand men, workers and military, later joined by a small contingent of WACs, releasing masses of bodily fluids year in and year out into the Northern Greenland waters were the initial cause of . . . global warming; in short, from this outpouring came the present problem confronting the entire Western Hemisphere—despite what scientists otherwise claim.

If ever there was any doubt that TRARG was the outside kid on the military block, our proximity to the dump merely confirmed its status. It was just a short hop "over there." Worse, inasmuch as the unit had been removed from the aluminum barracks and then squeezed into Atwells and tents, we had no septic tanks.

We had . . .

Outhouses! In Northern Greenland! Sans pits, again because of the permafrost.

Old-fashioned, rickety, wooden, tar-papered, outhouses! A total of two, count 'em, one for the enlisted men and the other—need it be identified? Naturally, we draftees gave the latter structure cachet by dubbing the latter Le Latrine Exclusive (LLE) for the officers, and Le Latrine Common (LLC) for us noncoms.

These were your typical nineteenth-century toilets, though obviously of wider dimension, a spacious one for the few officers, and for the peons, a primitive shanty structure.

Anything up there was fair game, even enemy paratroopers, but Le Latrine Common was our immediate, daunting, indisputable enemy. LLC was a two-level affair with an elevated throne, seven circular-shaped toilet-openings jammed against each other. Situated beneath each seat were sawed-off fifty-five gallon oil drums. Truly, an architectural marvel.

With the flimsiest insulation, no heating units, spaces between the boards to prevent suffocation, it was the challenge of our military careers and our future families.

And since the metal drums had to be removed every few days, the bottom rear-half of the structure was on hinges.

When the weather was calm it wasn't too bad, except maybe for the aroma that hung in like a steambath mist. Guys brought in reading material to pass the time of day, or if you will, daynight. Critics might dismiss our bitching by pointing out that while this was hardship duty, it was not Korea, and so we should just shut up. Right on!

Nonetheless this was the northern Arctic, and it may have been summer, but when the storms blew in and temperatures plunged and the wind cut through the nooks and crannies—especially in the gap below our asses—on such days no one save the occasional masochist could be seen with a magazine. The icy blasts produced a particular biological phenomenon, glassy gonads and frostbitten behinds. Single guys feared for their future begets.

Expediting one's needs as swiftly as possible was not only important, it was imperative. And there was no doubt about who had just been to the outhouse. Any guy running hell-bent along the rocky road simultaneously holding his balls and rubbing his rear end, we all knew he was not engaging in any kind of rite but trying to save his jewels. Threats sounded about filing for a Purple Heart: wounded in the course of bodily functions.

Yet there was another tricky part of the system, the problem of disposing of the putrid, brimming half-drums. This certainly called for the utmost creativity. The military solution: retrieve 'em, cart 'em, dump 'em. Right smack into Thule Bay.

To all campers familiar with this particular engineering finesse, the frequent runs to the coast became jauntily known as the "honeybucket detail." Twice a week, each and every (naturally) noncom got the assignment of trucking the drums to the highest hill overlooking the inlet, directed by a single (naturally) officer, who chatted cozily with the driver (naturally) inside the cab.

With the truck edged up to the perimeter of a high cliff, we noncoms scrunched down on our haunches, then swiftly and furiously shoved the drums out with both feet. The buckets sailed out into space as we cut loose with a "Geronimo." Who knows where the peculiar yell came from? Second World War paratroopers?

The half-cans momentarily floated in mid-air, then caromed downward along the hillside, smashing into the permafrost and shooting shit and piss high into the air. Lucky the detail when the wind was blowing in the opposite direction; luckier still when the stuff had solidified on the truck before it began its arced descent into the Arctic landscape.

All about Steve

C.O.: "Each Man Must Be Made to Realize That He Has a Vital Part to Play in the Mission"

He was for us draftees the ultimate in style and deliverance, yet we often sidestepped his insouciant quirkiness.

Athletically sculpted at six-foot-three, Steve's physical condition was only slightly off from his tight-end position at the football powerhouse, Michigan State University, and so every side courted him for the midnight volleyball game. So remarkable was Steve's athleticism that whether walking or running he gave the appearance of a gazelle in perpetual slow motion. What set him apart, though, was not his agility but an aloofness that no one could penetrate. At one time or another, most of us tried to pry him open to no avail.

Despite Steve's distancing posture, we were all drawn to his eccentricities. There was nothing cocky about him. He had a boyish grin that ran up his face and he never bragged about his gridiron feats. What really intrigued was his cold disdain for the military, which was somehow appropriate for our mission yet it just plain made things slightly more difficult for the rest of us. His attitude was not much more than many of us held; unlike anyone else, though, he had no fear of the brass, of anything that they could say or throw his way. It was as if his psychological immune system was impervious to military rewards and especially its multifarious punishments.

The brass truly loathed the man. He piqued their ire by falling out too slowly, reporting for duty too late, disappearing from camp too often, sometimes for many hours, or appearing deep in space too much. A familiar figure at sick call, he constantly moaned about a bad back, a sinus condition, a monstrous headache, a bum stomach. You name it, he had it. No one believed him, of course. He was just too much of a marvelous physical specimen. There was nothing they could do about it, but over time they came to suspect that he was a hypochondriac.

Rarely did he display animosity. Rather, Steve tiptoed amiability, his voice bordering on but never quite spilling over into apology. They made him a messenger boy, the lowliest of the low in the outfit. He silently glided through the arctic terrain as if he had never left the football field, tipping his hand to anyone he passed along the way, charmingly chattering with whomever.

Steve seemed to block out reality wherever he was, his way of maintaining an interior calm to offset whatever wrath might come his way. And it came his way all right, from the regulars all the way up the ladder to the C.O. Oddball actions not only set him apart from everyone, it was sometimes totally out of range.

Steve had ritualized each day's awakening at Fort Eustis, then in Thule, by guzzling down a can of beer. At the crack of dawn there was this awful sssiiinnnggg pop of a beer can being pried open, accompanied by hymnal gurgling. Once downed, this was followed by the arcing swoop of his arm as he nonchalantly directed, without aim, the empty can toward the metal garbage can yards from his bunk bed. Sometimes he got it right in, a bullseye, but far more often in his blurry-eyed state, a wide miss. Sharp claps reverberated throughout the morning silence as the can clanked around the floor. Inevitable cursing came from under the pillows. "Fuck off Steve, you goddamned biped, your throwing is as good as your catching at State."

That, in itself, was a bit much. But Steve was not finished with his early morning ablutions. As the can was hurtling toward the garbage bin, Steve would hoarsely deliver some salutation to Shakespeare: "'Dost thou think, because thou art virtuous, there shall be no more cakes and ale?' *Twelfth Night*, Act II, Scene III." Then shifting the covers back over his head, he would slip back into slumber.

Knowledge of poetry was not exactly unknown to the college guys in those days but athletes were another matter. We never did locate the origin of his habit. All we knew was that Steve possessed a true love for beer and the Bard. Libation and poetry were his greeting to himself, and in a strange way, to us. He only related that he had begun this ceremonial act shortly into basic training and would cease only after his incarceration in the military was over.

His lowly runner job suited him just fine. He was more than willing to accept a condition that for us would have been unthinkable. As we draftees rose up in rank, Steve was the only one mired in rank. He entered, and would leave the army, as a lowly private.

How many times did we hear the threats floating above the wind?? "Gammer, late again, where the fuck have you been!?" "Gammer, is your head on your goddamn shoulders?!" "Maybe your head is up your asshole!" "This time, Gammer, you're on latrine duty for the entire week!" "Gammer, I'm bringing your ass up on report! We've had enough of your fucking bellyaching and lame excuses!"

His replies only heightened their exasperation. Steve would slightly bow, and softly offer a "Hey, I'm sorry, really sorry, really I tried." Their response was automatic: "Your best is not worth shit, Gammer. This is it! I've had it! This time I'm writing you up on report, at the very least. Your balls will swing! Maybe even court-martial! Yeah!"

Ever so deferential, Steve would intone, "I understand what you're saying. I am laboring, truly."

But, no, he couldn't leave it just at that and invariably upped the ante. Whereas the phrase "court-martial" sent terror up and down us draftee spines, Steve threw it back, "If you really want to court-martial me, uumm, please tell me what are the charges!? Moving too slowly? Please, I'm going as fast as I can. My back's in pain and I have to lie down once in a while. Is there a regulation about forgetting to do something?" Then, the ultimate zinger, "Besides, I'm a private, there's nothing lower than me." Pausing, bending his torso low, he would offer up a Shakespearean line: "'Bow, stubborn knees,' *Hamlet*, Act IV, Scene V." There was nothing, nothing, they could do in the face of such resilient guile.

We marveled. Oh, to be so liberated!

Checking Out "C" Slope

Once, Steve's brazenness got the better of him. We were at the Nuna Takeoff Camp, and he was given a particular lamebrain assignment. It was a mildly crisp August day and the C.O. had been training his binoculars on an outlying receding snow range. Spotting a figure skiing down a small range, he turned to his aide, "Do we have someone testing 'C' slope this morning??"

"No, sir, I don't believe so, but maybe Major Hall is checking out the powder content."

"Yeah, could be . . . wait a minute . . ." The C.O. readjusted the range finder. "That man looks familiar." Leaning forward, he lowered and raised the glasses, exclaiming, "Son-of-a-bitch . . . looks like Gammer on that slope."

"Couldn't be," replied the aide, "he's down with a bad back. He's supposed to be walking paper around camp."

"Bad back? Again? Since when this time??"

"I think he showed up at Sick Bay yesterday."

"He's always at Sick Bay," snapped the C.O. "All I can say is that man out there had better not be Gammer. Not only will his back be hurting, his backside will be in a gargantuan sling. Here, take a look, who does this look like to you?"

The aide squinted through the binoculars. "Sir, I can't tell who the hell it is. Let's ask Major Hall."

"Okay, crank him up."

After a few minutes, the aide returned. "Sir, Hall says no one has been sent out today to 'C' slope."

"Bastard. That's Gammer sure as hell, and we got 'im this time. I want his ass in my quarters the minute he sneaks back into camp. Also, bring Boskin in. If this goes into the books, I want it recorded right."

Word spread quickly that Steve had been caught. This time there was no question of the Gammer-getting-the-hammer, as we joked, and sentenced to an ice cap court-martial. After a while, to be "gammered" meant just that in the outfit.

No sooner had he ambled back into camp than Steve picked up vibes of something being amiss. Maybe that was because a number of us rolled our eyes upward as we passed him heading toward his quarters.

Steve was ordered to the C.O.'s Atwell. "Private Gammer," said the colonel in a steely voice, "just where were you at 1425 hours?"

Steve spoke up with mushroomed sincerity. He knew he was caught and decided to brazen it out. "Sir, I was high up on slope 'C.'"

The C.O. was a bit rattled. He had expected some cockamamie story. "Slope 'C' eh? What the hell were you doing out there? According to Sergeant Mills, you were supposed to pick up the *Morning Report* and dispatch it to headquarters."

"Sir, I did dispatch the *Report* with my usual efficiency."

"Cut the crap, Gammer. You don't do anything speedily. Not here, anyway. I understand that you were in Sick Bay yesterday morning!"

"Sir . . . ?"

The C.O.'s sarcasm ratcheted up. "May I ask just why you were in Sick Bay, *Private*? Not that I really have to ask, do I!"

"Sir . . . my back . . . I had spasms upon awakening from a night of troubled dreams."

The C.O. doubled up. "More Shakespeare from you, Gammer, and I'll have you on latrine duty for the rest of your goddamn tour, do you understand? You can then quote all you want to the commodes. Spasms, huh, and then you decided that the cure was to ski down 'C' slope. And without permission, or a specific order? Is that right, Gammer?"

The C.O. was now getting into his high-gear anger. He looked directly at me. I knew he was very frustrated by the way the mission was going and wanted my understanding for the final report. I tried to convey simpatico but remained perfectly still, hoping that his diatribe would quickly run out of steam. So did Steve.

No way.

"Do you take me for an idiot, *Private*? Besides, I'm sure the Doc will be happy to hear that you prescribed your own treatment." A half-smile appeared on the C.O.'s face, "Yep, I'm real sure he'll testify in your behalf."

Steve maintained his composure. Not that he had much of a choice yet I was impressed. He just stood there, one cool dude. "Well, sir, you see, my back actually gets better when I'm able to move it around a lot, so I thought . . ."

The C.O.'s voice boomed out. He was incredulous at Steve's audacity. "Well, bully for you! I'm so delighted your own cure solves your ailment.

So much so that you took to 'C' slope for medicinal reasons! Oh my God. I want to remind you once again, Gammer, this is a top-secret operation, meaning twenty-four-hours-a-day until we return to the States, and in effect you went off without permission. That means," the C.O. paused to let the words sink in, "you went AWOL!"

The phrase ricocheted into my brain. AWOL is close to being treasonous. Even at this most serious challenge, Steve didn't even flinch. Rather, as I had seen him do many times before, he charged ahead. In a tone forceful and courteous, "Sir, do you want an explanation now, or at the hearing? May I quickly say in my defense—in the significant words of the mighty Shakespeare, 'To do a great right do a little wrong,' *The Merchant of Venice*, Act IV, Scene l."

This always threw them off kilter! For a long time I couldn't understand why. I doubt if Steve knew. Probably he had tried different approaches and this one simply worked. Was it in the offsetting incongruity of Shakespeare coming from an ex-football player, especially in this mind-boggling locale at the top of the world?

I mean, here we were in one of the world's most isolated settings, in a cramped Atwell butting up against the ice cap, the wind kicking up swirls of tundra dust, the air downright close to freezing, and an athlete, a private no less, is spouting Shakespeare to justify an unauthorized ski! How in God's fuck, I thought, did I ever get here? Did I really once covet this assignment!

At this latest challenge, I thought the C.O. would split a gut. For a moment or two he just looked at Gammer, clearly turning over in his mind some smart, proper military response. The momentary silence was just what Gammer was driving for, an exasperated C.O. I was dumbstruck when the C.O. fell for it.

"O.K., Gammer, let's hear your goddamned explanation. It'd better be good—no, wait, I'm sure it will be good! What I want to hear is how your act was in accordance with regulations, *Private*."

"I understand that, sir," Steve answered, his voice serenely earnest, "I would not give any excuse except in keeping with our military operation. May I preface my remarks with a previous civilian experience? You see, sir, as the coach at Michigan State always said, 'Boys, always remember, whatever you do on and off the field, you are a member of a team. You hear me! A team, and a very special one.'"

Steve had a focused look in his eyes, and not giving the C.O. a chance to cut in, quickly plowed ahead. "A team, the coach said, sir, 'is made up of all its parts and is only as strong as its weakest link.' Well, sir, that's always stayed with me, and . . ."

The C.O. just glared at Steve. "Oh, this is crap. Such crap! This is even beyond crap, it's sheer bullshit piled high and wide. I'm not interested in the churchly messages from your coach or your football days or Shakespeare, which we've heard too many times over the past months. Now, Gammer, directly to the point or this preliminary session is over and you're up on charges. You hear me!!"

Steve's head turned slightly sideways. "I wouldn't want to try your patience, Colonel. 'The quality of mercy is not strain'd, It droppeth as the gentle rain from heaven,' as the good Bard put it. I just want to show you how much I admired my coach at State, and you, sir, as my coach in the army."

"Oh for Chrissake, no more, and not another word from your Shakespeare!—or your coach!"

"Wait, sir, you see, I paid close attention to what you told us troops before leaving for Thule. You recall, sir, that you said TRARG is a team, that everyone has an essential part to play in this operation, no matter how small, and we all had to pull together."

The C.O. had a quizzical expression crossing over his eyes.

"You further said with fervor, sir, that this war would be won or lost by the smallest units in the military, that everyone has to give to his highest ability or else the enemy would be the ultimate victor."

That did it. "Ah, Gammer," said the C.O. in a tone slightly melodic, "you are no goddamn fool, that's for sure." Shaking his head, he started to laugh, "Nope, no fool are you—does that come from Shakespeare!? Now, what I reeallly want to hear is the connection between me, your so-called army coach, and 'C' slope. Are you saying that, in effect, that I directed you there, is that what we're getting at here?"

"Yes, sir, that's it, yes, that's it, you hit the nail all right," Steve said with much gravity, "everyone's task is to oversee the entire mission. Just like a football team at a game. Well, sir, I decided to test the powder on 'C' slope because there was talk among the glaciologists that it had become somewhat dangerous for our vehicles. I didn't want any of my buddies getting hurt if it was too soft. Turns out it's just right to be used by the tractor weasels. Sir, no problem there. I was about to report that to them when I was called in to see you, Sir."

"Gammer," the C.O. stood up shaking his head in wonderment, "you've tried my patience but I've got bigger problems—and assholes—to deal with these days. Don't let this happen again, because if you do, I promise—and this not for the report, Boskin—you will suffer. I will make you suffer in ways you've never thought of."

He paused before leaving the Atwell "One last thing, *Private*, you're a real card, a whole deck, I sure did need a little bullshit."

After, when I get back to the States, I thought, I've got to find a volume on Shakespeare. He must have written something about this episode. Sure enough, after rummaging through a bunch of plays, there it was:

He was for all a man, take him in all,
I shall not look upon his like again.

—*Hamlet,* Act I, Scene II

10

The Bet atop the World

Place: TRARG Mess Hall
Time: Late August, early evening
Weather: Gusty wind, 32 Fahrenheit

CHARACTERS

MASTER SGT. HANK "GADGET" TRESCA, Chief, Mess
Hall
PVT. STEVE GAMMER, Same Lowly Company Runner

Subject: Company Food

GADGET: Hey, got any more complaints, you so-called
biped athlete?!
STEVE: Gadge, this so-called corned beef hash is mish-
mash—it's Shakespeare's joke of the week.
GADGET: So laugh!
STEVE: Who can?! The hash is clogging my palate, it's
permafrost food.
GADGET: I bet your so-called Shakespeare would've
had somethin' to say about this, my ex-tight-end biped
from Michigan State. This so-called bard of yours, he had
somethin' to say about everythin.'

STEVE: Gadge, here's one for you: "Cloy the hungry edge of appetite by bare imagination of a feast." King Richard II, scene 3, line 289.

GADGET: When you get to be king, buddy boy, I'll serve you naked.

STEVE: Oh, Gadge, I always knew you were warm for my form. Let's sneak out to the fjord and silently slip away.

GADGET: Asshole!

The Crags

Not boredom, deprivation loosened the crags of craziness.

Deprivations simmered, and enlarged our fantasies. Over the expanding months we each began to salivate over one loss or another, real or imagined, it didn't much matter. Conversations became punctured with brusque sighs, explosive swearing, fists punched into the thin air, harsh expletives between us. What had seldom disturbed now singularly disturbed; what had barely piqued, now profoundly stretched; and what had been acceptable back in the States was abhorrent in the Arctic.

Guns were a point of friction. All the guys from Texas packed pearl-handled and crafted revolvers. Back at Fort Eustis, they had routinely cleaned and oiled them. Once in Thule, they accelerated the routine. Watching this almost nightly operation made us New Yorkers very, very fidgety. What with only seals and walruses, plus an occasional white bear cavorting around, what need could these guys possibly have for their diminutive shiny guns!?

Contrary to Chekhov's dictum—if you plant a pistol in act one, it'd better be fired by act three—there was only one ugly episode. An older regular, soused on bourbon, went berserk and waved his pistol at a group jiving him. His aim wasn't bad, he just had forgotten to load the thing. Shortly afterward he was ushered back to the States, amazingly the only company breakdown.

Another intriguing facet of Lone Star culture—entrancing, unnerving—was the good ol' boys' storytelling sessions. Only a Stephen Jay Gould could explain how evolutionary theory of natural selection produced

Texans as the best yarn spinners. Yet the flip side of their humor dispensed with crinkling eyes and broad smiles was a dark dimension. As Northeastern-bred novelist Norman Mailer once shrewdly observed, Texans possess "the scariest accent in America." On those days when those accented voices rose above the Arctic winds recounting tales and polishing their revolvers, we shuddered, and waited for whatever.

Not surprisingly, though, of all the yearnings sex was the thorniest, particularly for the married regulars. Mostly single, the draftees found it easier to sublimate. Beyond Sandi of whom I thought constantly, my own fantasies ran to several women I was in simultaneous correspondence with—and of course eventually screwed up by sending the wrong letter to one of them. She was so annoyed that she never let me forget it, and eventually married me.

Other aches pushed their way up with randomness, such as missing out on a newborn child, some downright peculiar taste like a Texas Hot, or some imagined jealousy. It wasn't hard to see in everyone's eyes at least a plaguing question or profound hankering. Mine revolved around future anxieties: was I smart enough to get a Ph.D.? would I ever get married? would I earn enough to support a whole family?

Then, like all such situations for which there is neither rhyme nor reason, an uproar occurred over a craving that no one, but no one, could have predicted. It led to a historical first in desserts and warfare, surely one of the oddest couplings in human behavior.

Gadget's Gamble

"What I wouldn't give for luscious strawberry ice cream," declared a loud voice in the company's small mess hall. Several draftee glaciologists and geologists drinking coffee were tackling some troublesome hurdles. "Fuckin' A!" said Gil. Other voices cheerily chimed in with flavors: "creamy pistachio," "cherry vanilla." Ron, hiding from crevasse patrol, kept it rolling, "Hey, don't forget butter walnut."

Flavors cascaded into a frieze of ice cream mirage.

No one had paid attention to Gadget, the domo mess sergeant, who sidled over to the table. "Hey, what're you guys in a lather about?"

Thickset, five-feet-eight, his well-rounded muscular stomach matched by a shiny bald head, a tough face made fiercer by slit eyes when he smiled, Hank Tresca was the guy with all the stripes. Eighteen years in service, he had earned the nickname because he described everything with the word, like, "Hey, how about that gadget!" But there was another interpretation that came closer to the nub of it, his prowess to fix any problem, anything at all, provided you were willing to pay his price for the fix. More dangerous requests upped his take. At such times, he was dubbed "GG" for the "Great Gadget." Openly smug about his brokerage skills, Gadget promoted his clout to any and all, including the officers.

You could banter with Gadget about his choice of mess menus or his intense poker playing, or even his misuse of the English language. He wasn't overly sensitive but he could spot a subtle putdown, and a perceived lack of deference made one's life miserable thereafter. Neither, though, could you be overly cowed by him because on occasion he offered much, much more than he could deliver.

So we draftees had sized him up as a shrewd guy whose actions carried weight when you needed him—for a steep price that few of us could afford in any case—but a little needling along the way was necessary.

The craving had almost melted away when a few older regulars came into the mess hall. "Hey, big regs, what kind of ice cream do you guys like?" geologist Don asked to stir up the ante.

"Yeah, a good question," one of the regular wiseacres chortled, throwing down the gauntlet to Gadget, "me, personally ah loves strawberry but all we get up here is watered down vanilla or cheap chocolate. How come we only get the scrawniest, an' then only two flavors? Isn't this supposed to be hardship duty? Haven't you ever heard of Howard Johnson's, Gadget? As mess king you should make our existence better."

"Yeah, Gadge, how come?" several of us draftees chimed in. "Our morale is shitty! We need different flavors. We could use some pistachio. How 'bout it?"

Gadget laughed, but we could see his eyes disappearing into their sockets. He had been challenged, not really by any of the draftees but by one of his own regulars. "So you guys want different kinds of ice cream, is that it? Up here in Greenland? Hey, I can provide it, but it'll take some time."

Calling for "some time" meant he was trying to save face. Nerves were frayed and we draftees just didn't want him off the hook. "How much time, Gadge?" Gadget stared into space. Voices filled the mess tent. "Hell, we know you're a goddamn genius about getting things done but this problem is probably beyond your talents. Yeah, it's allllrrright, really, we understand," exclaimed a regular.

"You cocksuckers," Gadget shot back, "hey, you guys think you're so fuckin' clever. But you don't mess with me, not for long anyhow. Hey, what's it worth to you all? How *much*? How much you guys be willin' to put inna pot that I can get you three, maybe four different flavors, say cherry, vanilla, strawberry, and pistachio. And great stuff—in two weeks' time. Yeah, just two weeks' time. How much, assholes??"

"Wait a minute, Gadge," declared the needling regular, "you want to bet you can provide the company with different flavors—in just a few weeks' time??"

"Yeah, that's what I'm saying. Hey, maybe I'll even throw in maple walnut or something like that just for kicks to show you guys who you're fuckin' around with!"

Everyone shouted figures. Gadget yanked out a pen and paper. When the din subsided, the outlines of a bet had been made. Tubs of ice cream filled with strawberries, cherries, nuts, marshmallows, the works in short, to be delivered at the mess hall at noon two weeks to the day. The odds jumped to 5–2 as Supply Rich became the broker, and took side bets.

As word of the bet spread to Nuna Takeoff Camp and the other isolated posts, everyone wanted in. Except for the officers, who were naturally excluded. If there was anything that brought the regulars and draftees in unspoken alliance, it was we versus them, as nice as several of them were, especially the former ROTC boys.

Giddy Fixation

Over the next several weeks the ice cream wager had everyone in the company hooked. In the pantheon of things, it was not just the ice cream that mattered, it was showing up Gadget, making him eat his words so to speak, that mattered even more.

Nothing else had priority, either. No one gave a damn about the B-52s with their nuclear loads on their way to or from the outer reaches of the Enemy. Screw the stupid-ass MIGs! Screw also the weariness of mission ups-and-downs, of round-the-clock efforts and relentless sunup to sunups.

Counting up the pot, we knew that Gadget stood to lose at least $400, a princely sum in those days. A private first class salary stood at $76 per month before subtracting withholding plus the life insurance policy. We also realized that he stood to gain a lordly sum but that possibility was dismissed: "No fuckin' way!"

Whether directing meals at the hall or plunging the poker games, Gadget was constantly needled. Hands, palms up, or open wallets, everyone asked him to fork over their part of the bet. "Gadge, why wait? Gadge, save yourself embarrassment."

"Think you're funny, you bastards," he lashed back, "you'll soon be eating crow before I'm finished." He knew it was a mistake as soon as he said it because the retort was swift. "Hell, Gadge, I'd just as soon have a lovely bunch of ice cream, thank you!"

Shortly thereafter, though, his demeanor changed, and a sweet, almost syrupy smile came across his face, something akin to a Loony Tune character, or was it Count Dracula? We knew something was up and tried to figure it out. What was the bastard scheming? He had put himself into that unenviable place where you either put up or shut up. After assessing the situation, regulars and draftees alike concluded that he was bluffing, angling for a face-saving way out.

If Gadget was seeking an honorable escape, it was a mistake. Almost no one was willing to let him off the hook, not even his regular buddies. It might have been different back in Virginia, but up here nerves were nearly as glacial as the ice cap. A bet is a bet, and he was out to lose a hell of a lot: "Tough shit!"

Giddiness overtook the company as the days trekked down to the moment of deliverance. Five days had slipped swiftly by. Even though the MIGs were coming in almost every week sending our fighter jets swwooo- osshing to scare them off, we couldn't care less. All that mattered was savoring the sweetness of having Gadget's nickname dethroned. Well, that was not the only thing, the money mattered too, an awful lot at stake.

Then, on the day before the agreed deadline, we suddenly noticed that Gadget was nowhere to be seen. He had disappeared.

AWOL in Thule!?

Calls went out. We scoured the compound area, nothing doing there. We rang up Camp Takeoff. Every report of his whereabouts was negative. His assistant was overseeing the mess hall. Was Gadget in hiding or just skunk-drunk? We had no doubt that he was going out of his wits. Maybe he had checked into the psychiatric ward at the base hospital claiming to be in need of R&R? We placed an oblique call there.

That evening abounded with expletives. He was, among other things, "a stupid prick," and the worst, "a chicken-shitting coward." "I never thought he would chicken out," said a regular, "finesse it, yeah, but bug out, no way, son-of-a-bitch!" As the night wore on, still no trace. Where could he be hiding?

"Wait a minute," said buddy Dave vehemently, he and Tom not gloating, "what if maybe, just maybe, something has really happened to Gadge, that he hasn't bugged out?" All of a sudden we were in a panic, guilt pouring out of us. What had we done here? Judging Gadget when he might well be hurt, and lord knows where! Dividing into groups, we undertook a serious hunt, no problem because the sun stayed right where it was supposed to be. Looking under and behind buildings, around the nearby hills, searching the dump, nothing. Not everyone joined in, though. Supply Rich offered bets that he had weaseled out because he was way over his head on this one. At 1 a.m. we called it quits.

Now the officers who were privy to the bet but pissed at being excluded got into the act. The C.O. sent word down that if Gadget was not back in the mess hall by lunchtime on the following day, precisely when the buckets of ice cream were due at the base, he was prepared to report him missing and bring in the air force police. "If that bastard is not missing but hiding out somewhere," the C.O. avowed, "I'm going to have his ass on AWOL report."

AWOL in Thule, Greenland? It sounded too hilarious to us draftees. Every soldier throughout the military had to be accounted for in the

Morning Report, the official record of everyone's comings and goings that went out each and every morning of the year to ten different locations throughout the military hierarchy. What would the *Report* conjecture? "Top Sergeant Hank Tresca went over the Westenholme fjord and onto the ice cap?" or "Hitched onto an iceberg going south into the North Atlantic where he was picked up by a Norwegian fishing boat?"

High Noon

Almost no work was accomplished that morning. Foreboding mixed with bewilderment. If not hurt or dead, Gadget was certainly up for disciplinary action. Top-secret missions were not taken lightly by the military, especially with the MIGs increasing their surveillance flights and Moscow Molly haranguing us. By pulling the entire outfit into its orbit, the intensity of the bet had obviously rankled the C.O.

The clock ticked slowly down, as it did for Gary Cooper in *High Noon,* only no vengeful Russians were due at the compound. Only tubs of ice cream, which did not seem possible short of a miracle.

At noon, the air base's siren sounded as it did every day. We all moved outside to scan the main road that curved at an almost ninety-degree angle into the camp. Nothing.

Then came the faint grating sounds of vehicles along the hard pebbled road. The sounds grew larger. Abruptly rounding the corner into the compound came several loader trucks bearing air force insignias. Air force vehicles??

And there in the lead vehicle sat Gadget grinning from ear-to-ear. Wide-eyed and speechless, we all stood fixed in place. As the first truck headed hell bent for the mess hall, the window opened and Gadget leaned half-way out, shouting, "You fuckers! Pay up, pay up!"

Only our heads and eyes moved as the trucks whizzed by.

Like a herd of wildebeest, we suddenly broke into a run after the trucks, yelping and whooping. "That unbelievable bastard," exclaimed Dave admiringly, "he pulled it off after all. Now he'll be impossible to live with. How in the world did he do it?"

He was already standing on a chair behind a small table in front of the mess hall. His round, pool ball head bobbed back and forth. "Hey, what've we got here!? It sure is good to see you guys but I don't think you're too happy to see me! Nah! But it's time to wrap this up. Yeah! All right, line up with your bucks. Then go inside and you can have your choice of any— that's right, you heard me you shits—any of five, count 'em, five flavors to choose from! And don't ask me how!! I ain't tellin' or talkin'—unless," he snickered, "except maybe for another fiver. You can have one scoop, hear—as large you want!"

Inside the mess hall were about twenty small containers with various flavors. We each filled our bowl to the brim and walked out into the Arctic sunshine, savoring the most delicious ice cream, ever. Some of Gadget's favorite boys scrounged seconds. Rich got away with another bowlful.

Buttering up the Mess Sergeant

Over the next couple of weeks there was constant musing over how Gadget had accomplished the impossible. Chortling as he went around the area, piquing the college boys at every opportunity, Gadget relished his mini-speeches: "Fuckin' graduate degrees in electric engineering and geology and math, even a goddamn historian whatever the fuck he does, and none of you bastards can figure it out?! Hey, just shows you don't need an education to be smart." As Dave had warned, he was impossible to live with.

So we waited, and believe me, we plotted. Sooner or later Gadget would spill out his tale, but only after he had won big at a poker session or was spiked with booze, or both. Sure enough, about a month after the episode he did pretty well at the game, plus was riding high on the bourbon. Pretty tipsy as he was, though, Gadget still had his antennae up. However, we had also prearranged a surefire maneuver, heaping flattery on him in unctuous rhythms.

"Gadget," Steve started off with awe in his voice, "you really pulled off a big one, and we humble draftees congratulate you. Not only did you pull it off, you made suckers out of us."

"Fuckin' A, I really did—but you ain't goin' get me to tell you how."

"Nope, we figure you'll never tell," said Gil matter-of-factly. "We just want you to know that our admiration for you has soared. You're smarter than most experts we know."

"Fuckin' A right, you'd better believe it."

I chimed in. "In fact, Sarge, it's best that we don't know. Makes what you did all the more amazing."

"Hey, when you think of it, it was pretty good, yeah, probably one of the best—nah—by far the best I ever pulled."

"Tell us about the others, Gadge, what were they like?"

"Sure, I'll tell about 'em."

It looked as if our plan had failed. Gadget could really put away the sauce, and most of us were pretty blotto as well. Then he shook his head, and grinned, "Nah, why should I tell you those? The best is the best, so fuck it, why not? Hey, we're soon gonna be outta this cold dump, so it can't hurt. I think the air force guys are somewhere else by now, anyway. But I don't want no blabbin' mouths in any case, especially to the fuckin' officers, certainly not the C.O. You guys hear me!?"

Dealer's Hand

"Air force? Right, you had their trucks!" I exclaimed. "What did they have to do with it?"

"Hey, always the historian . . . Almost everything, and they extracted their price too. Everybody all the time wants something. Don't matter what the action is." Peering over at Rich, a coy smirk cut across his face. "Hey, sure you guys really wanna know!?"

"Cut the shit, Gadget," exclaimed Rich, a bit miffed, "and tell us how the fly boys were in, and how much you had to pay them?"

Gadget swigged his glass empty, then giddily spat it out. "Okay, I'll lay it for you pricks, slow and simple. First, the easiest was getting the stuff, you know the fruits, nuts, syrups. Remember the navy ship, the icebreaker *Westwind* that was in port at the time? Hell, the navy supplies its guys with fresh stuff all the time. So I swung by and picked up large cans of cherries, pineapple, peaches, and syrups on the QT. The quartermaster made out like a bandit but I didn't care. I knew I would make it back, in spades. The nuts and the salt were easy. I requisitioned them from the air force quartermaster, told 'im it was the C.O.'s birthday and wanted to bake a couple of large cakes so the company could celebrate. They were only too happy to *ac-comm-o-date* . . ." he mouthed the word very slowly, "hey, you college lads know the meaning of that word!?"

He slowed down a bit. "Now, the cream, hey, that was the toughest thing to get. All we got up here in this God forsaken place is that powdered shit, like eggs 'n' milk. Can't use powdered anything for ice cream. I was stuck until I got wind of a bunch of bigwinded congressmen coming to see how we're doing up here. Only they never con-de-scend—how's that college word, heh!—to visit us troops. They always stay at the posh suites at Hilton Thule and write their reports through binoculars." The "Hilton Thule" crack brought down the tent.

"Well, I got the idea of calling up the air force PR boys. I told 'em we'd like to throw a party for the dignitaries—if their schedules permitted. But we're gonna need lots of milk and cream to make special cakes and coffee. Hey, the bigwigs might not come then again they might and wouldn't it be nice if we had it all arranged beforehand? The air force would get all the credit. Hey, that PR guy fell all over himself, thankin' me for our consideration and shipped over wads of containers. 'Course I knew the fuckin' bigwigs wouldn't show. So by the end of the week I had all the ingredients and the containers. Well, that's it, lads, that simple!"

He poured himself another hefty drink. A bunch of us grabbed for the bottle, now quickly emptying. "Gadge, you're a genius," said Dave. "We'll never question you again about your vast accomplishments." Gadget's smile went up several notches.

"Still, something's missing here." Don, shrewd geologist that he was, piped in softly but firmly.

"What's that?" replied Gadget tightly. "I told you everything!"

Don was annoyed. None of us said a word. "Cut the crap. I used to make ice cream at home. My folks taught us how to prepare it, and the toughest part was getting the ingredients to harden. My brothers and I would take turns cranking that lever around and around in the tub until our arms fell off. Feel this muscle," he leaned into Gadget, "it came from turning that bar hundreds of times."

Gadget gave him a wary grin. Don revved up the monologue. "Now, just how did you get that cream to harden? If you had lots of time, that's one thing. All you had to do was leave it in a large subzero refrigerator. But if you got the stuff together at the last minute, like you say, then you got a problem. How'd you get it so smooth and hardened in such a short time?"

"Hey, you got me, college asshole." Gadget thrust a hand upward. "It was a stroke of genius, if I say so myself." He stopped, circled the tent with his eyes, and then said gravely, "What I got to say goes no further than this outfit, and if ever I'm called in to explain anything—anything, I'll deny it—and then the chicken-shit who blabbed will wish he were in the middle of the fuckin' ice cap with only his jock strap on. You hear me!?"

His fierce tone made me wince. Then he looked straight at me, pointing a finger, "And nothing about this in the fuckin' weekly report and not the history of this screwed up mission either—hey, buddy boy!"

I took the threat to heart—until now.

Ice Cream Combat!

"Ah, those Russians," Gadget smiled, "God bless 'em, they saved my beautifully formed ass."

Everybody went quiet. "The Russians?!?"

"Sure. You know how those MIGs been flyin' over the base more than ever? Well I figured—nah, prayed—that they would come sometime soon before the deadline."

Now I jumped in. "Gadge, get to the point. You were hoping that the Russian planes would set off an alert??"

"College shits, will you ever shut up! Well, about a month ago I was over talkin' to my air force buddy at his mess hall and a couple of jet pilots were there havin' coffee and doughnuts. So I sat down with 'em and bullshitted. Found out lots of interesting things like how long it takes 'em to get into the air and back again, how much capacity they carry, and all kinds of stuff."

This intrigued the technicians who wanted to know just how long it took the catapulted fighter jets to swing into action from their hangers. "Hey," Gadget protested, "I'm runnin' around tryin' to get all the ice cream ingredients together with time running real low and all you shits want to know is about the fighter jets? Fuck you," he growled.

We quickly got him back on track.

"Let me tell you, there wasn't enough time to get the stuff to . . . to congeal—hey, lads, another good word!—when it hit me. I rung up my buddy and told 'im my problem. He thought I was out of my fuckin' mind but asked how he could help. Hey, I said, could he arrange a deal with the pilots? I said they would all get a piece of the action. Sure, he replied, and we got together and struck a bargain."

We all sat mystified. What, we wondered, did the pilots want out of the deal? "Fuck," said Gadget, "all the fly boys asked for maybe a little betting mazuma plus some ice cream! Can you picture that!! So they agreed to remove some of the shooting hardware and jam ice cream cans into their spaces. All the ingredients were in there, all mushy, and I needed them hard as a rock. Then when the MIGs came taking their stupid-assed pictures, the fly boys took off as usual, chased 'em for a short ways, and came back. Only this time they had ice cream in their bellies, frozen solid."

We sat stupefied, barely anyone drinking. Gadget didn't even notice. "Hey, I got lucky, boy did I get lucky, sometimes you need lady luck. Fuck, even I know that." He paused for a moment, looked around the group, making sure that we all understood how smart he was, and how luck had smiled on him.

"Yeah, can you believe it," he repeated for our benefit, "the MIGs came over just before the deadline—the jets boys took off with twenty-four cans—hell, in minutes they were all were Arctic frozen. Maybe they were up for ten minutes. When they parked their planes back in the hangers, I was waitin' with open arms. I stored them in my buddy's freezer units, hopped into a bunk for a short nap and high-tailed it here. Hey, a piece of cake . . . no, make that ice cream!"

He let out a roar of a laugh. "Pricks!"

Shades of Willie and Joe (Again)

For a solid week the talk was about Gadget's great ploy. Envisioning cans of ice cream in fighter jets chasing Soviet planes across the top of the world was too much, topping even the bizarre goings on constantly plaguing our mission.

Surrealism touched again a few days later when some guys came running into the compound yelling about the moon: the MOON, the MOON! LOOK LOOK! For five months we hadn't seen any darkness or stars, only the sun reaching out in an ever-widening circle. Cries of the MOON brought out the entire camp with cameras snapping furiously, each of us intent on capturing the delicious moment. Back in the States, showing slides to friends and relatives brought forth yawns. "It's only the moon," they declared. "No, you don't understand," I would forcibly repeat, "it's the MOON, don't you get it!" They never did.

Eventually, the topic petered out as logistical problems superseded and the normal snafus continued. But just before we broke away from a late night drinking session, Gil shoved his glass high into the air. "To Gadge, yeah, to Gadge, I drink to you not only for a brilliant stroke but because you probably achieved a first in military history. Isn't that right, Joe?" I wondered what he was getting at, and not wanting to appear too dense, sort of nodded. "To the world's most expensive ice cream!" Gil had clearly given it some thought. And he wasn't finished.

He pulled out a piece of paper, and began reading, deliberating, emphasizing his points. "The way I figure it, give or take a few dollars here and there, if you compute the cost of shipping all the ingredients from the States, throwing in the navy's contribution, adding the jet fuel, the fly boys' pay, and the time spent by the company screwing around about it, each vat of ice cream cost about $2,500, the total for twenty-four cans coming to about $60,000." We sat mesmerized.

And let out a whoop. Gil put up his hand. He had more to come. "Gadget said he gave four cans to the pilots. We shared twenty. Each can produced about ten large scoops. That means each scoop of ice cream cost a whopping $250. I repeat, two-hundred-and-fifty dollars! Now, that's pretty steep, in fact, outrageous."[1]

Dave and I glanced at one another. Over the many months, we had become convinced of the pointlessness of the mission, and furious at the way it had been organized. It was just plain reckless all the way around. A total waste! We shared a conviction that the so-called defense budget was ruining social programs, and that the Cold War had narrowed political discourse. On more than one occasion we had gotten into heated discussions in the PPP over these issues, especially with the regulars over the dastardly tactics of Republican Senator Joseph McCarthy of Wisconsin.

We were definitely in the minority in the outfit but there were several others. Constantly infuriated by the cost and mismanagement, a small number of us draftees threatened disclosure. We singled out certain congressmen we would write to, and thought about composing a group piece. We knew, though, that between the Korean War and McCarthyite oppression, it would be near impossible to turn anything around.

Gadget reached in to continue the discussion. "Hey, yeah, a bit steep," he nodded. "But, fuck, think of it this way, the joke was on the Russians bein' chased by jet fighters filled with ice cream. Shit, this is a war we're in. Anything goes."

Anything goes! The wizened Dealer had spoken. We nodded wearily. What the hell, the initial phase of the mission was almost over and eventually we would be heading back to civilized Fort Useless. As offended as we were over the figures, it did strike us at the time that probably never again would ice cream taste as luscious as it did at high noon in exiled Thule.

11

Whirling Dervishes

Requests ...

In mid-May, the thick ice covering the fjord cracked, forcing the convoys to hustle even more swiftly across the dangerous, rising waters until finally the ice road out to Takeoff Camp slid speechlessly under. Then the burden of transporting every manner of thing and personnel from Thule fell to the Helicopter Division. This monumental task was made even more difficult by the fact that there were only five or six machines at any given healthy moment. Four were H-19s, a lumbering vehicle capable of hauling tonnage over long distances, and several were H-13s, a lightweight aircraft seating two encased in a circular plastic bubble.

Because it was so pivotal, the Helicopter Unit was special, blue-blood army, manned by a substantial force. The choppers were also used to reconnoiter the changing ice terrain in search of the elusive crevasses. So, all in all, the mission could not possibly even hope to succeed without the division, and since time was a precious lode it had to be in tip-top shape.

Of course, the helicopter boys were fully attuned to their weight because as the saying goes, if you've got it, flaunt it. They didn't hide their cockiness one bit.

Especially did the pilots delight in the H-13s. Then they really strutted or rather whirled their stuff. Throughout the summer requests for the machine poured in. Visiting military and congressional voyeurs requested observation trips. Any field-grade officer, any congressional overseer, no matter the big-shot, had his request granted. Off they went into the wild Arctic yonder with their Leica cameras snapping away since this was the main reason for their requests.

9. H-13: nauseous nemesis.

Is it necessary in this crazy-quilted history to state that these requests made a mockery of the mission by subverting schedules and intelligence secrecy? And shouldn't it also be said, despite no one giving a hoot in hell, then or now, that costs ratcheted way up as a result?

Every visitor coveted the H-13s because this machine came so close to the fantasy of Aladdin's magic carpet. Sailing along at only several hundreds of feet above the Thule fjord and ice cap, the whirling bird offered a stupefying panoramic view of massive icebergs caroming away from the ice cliffs into the sea, of dark crevasses looming against serene whiteness, of silver-blue streams gushing into the fjord, of an expanse of sky flowing all the way to nowhere—provided, of course, the winds were friendly, the whiteouts anticipated, the machines in tip-top shape, and the helicopter boys not too sloshed from the night before. Prayers often accompanied the big payloads.

Betty and *The Cyclone*

Heady as it was for others, the air-sail thrill of a lifetime was not for me. I was already quite content defending my country as a land historian. I did not request such a flight on the H-13, did not want it, and when so ordered protested all the way to the C.O., then practically died on the flight. This is almost a posthumous memoir.

Ever since a couple of older boys on my block threatened to heave me off a five-story apartment building—would you believe in later years several became lawyers specializing in corporate merger law—I have possessed the utmost respect for heights. Which is to say total and abject fear.

Things were so far behind schedule at the Takeoff Camp that every available body was shipped over. Since I had to compile and file on deadline the status reports, I thought—actually, fervently prayed—I would remain immune from this excursion into utter chaos.

Alone at my typewriter ardently concentrating on a love letter, I sensed a presence. The C.O.'s aide was looming over me. "Boskin, get your ass 'n gear, in that order, you're going over."

"Sir?"

I jumped up before he had a chance to look down at what I was doing. "I know how bad it is at Takeoff Camp but I just cannot fly on any of those machines. I'm petrified of heights. No bullshit, I'm truly and unequivocally petrified! Can't I work on problems here??"

"Boskin, cut the crap. You heard the colonel. Everyone has to go this time. This mission's in deepshit trouble—and keep in mind that this assessment is not for the report!"

"I hear," I grumbled, "I hear you loud and clear."

The worse things became the more I heard this despairing edict uttered by upper echelon officers. The brass was getting antsy about the concluding history of the mission. And I, in turn, was developing an icky paranoia about their intentions. Was this order to Takeoff Camp an example of intimidation, or designed to do me in?

"Major, there's no question in my mind that I will die on that flight. Then there'll be no one to write the history about this memorable top-secret operation."

"Balls, Boskin, good try." He let out a short chortle. "You and I know, do we not, that there's always someone to take your place! Yeah, Boskin, they may not be as good as you . . . hmmm, at least I assume you are. Listen up, somewhere in this goddamn army there's another historian, hell, probably dozens of 'em for all I know." His voice stiffened, "So get your gear pronto-pronto and be out at the pad by 1400 hours."

I was half-tempted to ask him if the "irreplaceable" theory also applied to him, but held back. I could see that arguing wouldn't work. At the very least, though, I would attempt to improve my chances of survival. "Sir, if I really have to go over, I would like to request traveling on the big H-19s. That one with the tiny bubble frightens me."

"Ah, Boskin," the aide smiled, "you do try. No such luck. Nope, I'm afraid you're going to have to bite the bullet, so to speak. It's just you and Captain Maroon, on his favorite flying machine, the H-13."

My mouth opened so quickly that he let out a howl. Making a swift beeline to the C.O.'s Atwell, I knocked and pushed the door open before he even had a chance to invite me in. Poor guy. I didn't give him much of a chance to say anything.

"Colonel, I know we've been at odds about the history but while I take that seriously I have a higher regard—my life! Sir, my terror of flying in the H-13 helicopter is all Betty's fault." I thought introducing her at this juncture would pique a laugh, and maybe even save my ass.

He pushed back his chair, cocked his hand into the shape of a gun, and bellowed, "Bang." I quieted down. "Now if you don't want me to reach for a real weapon, you'd better slide your hide outta here. I'm way too busy for your nonsense . . . who in hell is Betty?"

Betty! I poured out the tale about how my supercharged teenage love had over and again teased my masculinity when I steadfastly refused to go with her on that awesome roller coaster in Coney Island, *The Cyclone.* I was not alone in my terrifying appraisal of "the beast." Charles Lindbergh, the first to fly miraculously nonstop across the Atlantic Ocean in a single-engine plane in 1927, had actually exclaimed that *The Cyclone* was even more exciting than that voyage. I suppose Lindbergh possessed a wry sense of humor.

On this issue, I didn't! I silently screamed the minute the minicars left the dock, went up ever-so-slowly on the track to the top and then plunged— yes, *plunged* ninety degrees, I swear, down the other side. Yes, I did scream out loud. That horrifying jaunt seared itself like a branding iron into my consciousness.[1] It took me weeks to recover and in retrospect I don't think my reputation with Betty ever did. Looking cheerfully sinister, the C.O. comically waved me away with his hand. Now I was even more convinced they were out to get me!

The Ulcerous One

The gods were not with me! It wasn't just the dreaded H-13, it was also that Captain Dock Maroon, the officer with whom I had had a bad spat not more than a week before, was the pilot.

Second-in-command of the Helicopter Division, Captain Maroon was a slim, acidic, tight-lipped man who had lived with ulcers the major portion of his life. He even had a portion of his stomach removed for this condition. When in a particular sour frame his well-known proclivity was to bellow at any question, no matter how civil, his voice rising above the wind. Given the intricate, high-strung helicopters, I had him pegged as not exactly your ideal pilot. Or, for that matter, someone you could throw an innocuous inquiry, which unfortunately I did one day.

"Captain, when you see Major Hall at Takeoff Camp, I wonder if you could remind him that the status report is due tomorrow!?" I had had problems with him all summer.

"Damn that report," Maroon shouted, "why do you keep changing the day when it's due?"

"Now, sir, nothing's changed . . ."

"Besides, that report is not due till Friday and here it is only Wednesday. You're bugging us again!"

"But, sir, today's Thursday . . ."

"Today," Maroon was really getting into it, his bile churning deep within the remaining portion of stomach, "is not Thursday, Corporal, no it is not THURSDAY, damn you—the section has always handed the report in on time."

To contradict him would be futile so I acceded to his error. "All I want, sir, is to remind . . ."

"REMIND! You goddamn pencil pushers—you never seem to get things right!"

At this point, a regular, bless him, quietly put a calendar in front of his face, pointing out the day. Maroon squinted, also not a good sign for a pilot. "Thursday, eh?" His voice dropped an octave or two. "My heavens, where do the days go? Well, well . . ." He was about to offer some slight apology, then caught himself. Not a good thing to do before the lowly. Up an octave went the words. "Weeell, Corporal, it doesn't make any difference what day it is or isn't, that status report is always handed in on time. End of discussion!"

"Yessir, I only wanted . . ." The door closed tightly as he abruptly departed.

To Puke or Not to Puke . . .

He was waiting for me as I alighted from the Jeep, a broad smile stretched across tight eyes. What was he smiling about? Did he know of my flying fright? Had the colonel clued him in during a moment of sadism?

"Weeell historian," the voice was chirping, "ah, we meet again. Here to remind me that the report is due this Friday!? Let's see, what's today, Sunday, isn't it? Just think, we have just five days before we get static from you."

Behind him was the helicopter with that infernal, miniscule, plastic see-through bubble, my nemesis, the H-13! I was too stricken to offer a reply.

"Okay, here's the deal. Have you ever flown in the H-13?" I didn't utter a sound. "No, I guess not, or so the C.O.'s aide said."

Uh-oh, so that was the bastard who squealed. That meant the entire company had heard by then.

"Sooo," he continued merrily, "first step, strap your gear in that little compartment and put on this helmet. Now," he opened up a small door on the bubble, "slide in and strap yourself across your lap and chest and get your sunglasses out." I did, as ordered. And was no sooner strapped in that I wanted to cry out, plead, promise him anything, anything that would put a stop to my instant demise.

The bubble was even smaller than small! It was microscopic!! I put out my hands to touch it. Barely an arm length! Plus the seats were no more than inches apart. He grinned at me as he started the engine, the blades turning sluggishly, then faster, then ear-plunging noisy.

Still not a sound had outed from my riveted lips. But questions ricocheted from my head to my stomach: Was he now going to get even with me? Am I going to be jettisoned from this accursed bubble? Suddenly the questions stopped. It occurred to me that Maroon was in his element! That's why he flew, to get away from the earthly acids that filled his half-stomach. He was a prime example of that species that didn't belong on the ground.

Now I kept my eyes riveted shut. *Swwwoooosssshhhh* . . . The craft headed straight up forcing my eyes open, my mouth ajar. I peeked, petrifyingly, out. Only the plastic separated me from toppling out and I was convinced it was only a short time before it dissolved!

Maroon was humming, paying no attention to me, just checking his instruments, purring on. I was so grateful that he held no spite. Grateful for the weather that was picture perfect. Keeping my head locked in position, lips narrowed, I choked out "nice weather" to him.

With great effort I glanced down, and as quickly grabbed for my seat. ANY MOMENT NOW, I recited to myself, RIGHT OUT! Below me was the green-white fjord filled with seals caroming around dozens of icebergs. Looming ahead were the outer cliffs of the ice cap itself, which even from the height of a thousand feet appeared beautifully foreboding, a serrated white cover with several blue waterfalls running down to the sea.

Suddenly the craft plunged vertically down! Maroon stopped humming. My eyes grabbed for their sockets and my innards turned mushy. I was barely breathing when I heard him humming again, muttering something like . . ."I'm telling you Boskin your damned reports are no damned good . . . well, that was a damned good example of a downdraft . . . happens all the time . . . weather looking good don't mean it's good . . . sometimes it's even worse when we HAVE TO EVADE, LIKE THIS . . ."

This time my voice didn't fail me. I let out a shriek as the craft headed diagonally toward the ice cap. The bastard was getting EVEN.

"Youwin youwin!!!" I hollered.

"What did you say?" Maroon said merrily as he steered the craft up and to the left toward Takeoff Camp.

Right then I felt as if all the food I had eaten in the past week was going to splatter the see-through bubble. He spotted it through the corner of his eyes. "No fuckin' way, Corporal," came a determined firm voice, "put your head between your legs and pray that you don't puke in *my* machine 'cause if you do I'll have you cleaning this 'copter for the next month."

A mighty struggle ensued between head and gut, between allowing the natural and fearing the natural. The last thing I wanted was to become Maroon's bile slave. I kept my head locked between my legs, eyes closed, and concentrated all my thoughts on blocking my stomach from its appointed desire. I stayed that way for what seemed like hours. Then I heard humming again and knew it was safe to unlock my knees.

In less than ten minutes we were down at Takeoff Camp. Maroon's grin was gone. Once back on the ground he started hollering at the guy tethering the 'copter. He was back in his acidic state, poor fellow.

Dubious Triumph

From the beginning, the Helicopter Division laid logical claim to company's complex priorities. Fulfillment or failure rested squarely on a handful of whirling blades. Yet the cost of giving in to what they wanted was a harbinger of how things were going to turn out, meaning half-badly.

Even from the early political maneuverings of who-gets-what-and-where, the helicopter boys emerged triumphant. Their headquarters should have been at Camp Takeoff, the staging area where virtually all the crucial ice cap experiments occurred. Even the C.O. wanted it in that location.

However, the pilots had been billeted at the air force officer quarters suites, which were replete with hot showers, bar, billiards, and lord knows how many other hidden perks. Moving them across the fjord to the primitive Takeoff encampment would have meant the pilots relinquishing their posh quarters at Thule's equivalent of the Hilton. "Fuck NO!" they were recalled as saying to the C.O. when he ordered their removal from Thule's posh to Takeoff's desolation. War is hell, but there is no reason to have to go there.

The C.O. stood his ground. His order was intractable. Sipping scotch in their suites, the equally unbending helicopter pilots plotted another strategy. It would take time to get all its various components together, they told the C.O. They would certainly begin preparations, they informed him, but how much time, they couldn't calculate. Box score: Helicopter boys 1, C.O. 0.

Dutifully bound, I described the imbroglio in the status report. Tactfully—or so I thought—the logistical insanity not to locate the Helicopter Unit at camp was specified. Other pertinent sections had been relocated to Take-Off Camp, so it was imperative that the main transportation unit in TRARG be situated where it made the most sense for the overall mission.

Not long after transmitting the report to the C.O., I was summoned to his Atwell. Another skirmish was about to begin.

"Ah, B-o-s-k-i-n," said the C.O. deliberately, his irritated way of shutting off any exchange, "just where's your head at these days!"

"Sir?"

"Hey, don't bug me, B-o-s-k-i-n, just answer the question!"

I knew what was coming and sought for the right reply, one that wouldn't provoke him any further. In a flash I recalled my old debating coach's sage advice at Oswego: "When in doubt, answer a question by using the wording of the question itself."

"Sir, just where should my head be at?"

He looked at me, shaking his own head vigorously.

So much for an old debating technique.

"I'll tell you where it's at, Corporal, hanging between your legs. And I'll tell where we will both be—under the guillotine, that's where—just in case you had any doubts! Hey, how's my sense of history!?"

"Too good. Sir, look, I think I know what you're getting at."

"Do you now? Think!? Well, then, what the hell did you THINK you were doing when you included this particular conflict in the report! Is this déjà vu, or didn't we have this very conversation weeks ago? Have you plain forgotten what I said THEN about reporting internal squabbles!!"

"Colonel," I turned to title for effect and to appeal to his sense of importance, "this report goes to the pros in the Pentagon and they expect some degree of professionalism. If we snow them with platitudes, they're sure as hell to get suspicious. Better to throw in a conflict now and then."

I paused for a moment, and shifted the argument. "But I must admit I have an additional reason for mentioning the situation. Colonel, if the Helicopter Unit gets its way, all indications are that it's going to be tough to accomplish what this mission's all about. All the other sections are saying the same thing." It felt good playing military strategist.

Not to him. He also turned to title for effect. "Corporal, I can't believe this bullshit I'm hearing," he said in short breaths. "Since when did you become a military strategist?! You're a goddamn historian, keep that in mind at all times from here on. Where in hell did you hear that the mission was doomed if the Unit remained in Thule??"

I didn't hesitate a minute. I wasn't about to play the no-sources game. "From Major Antonelli, sir. He was talking about it to Captain Doc"—the name we gave to the unit's medical officer—"in Sick Bay the other day. The major was giving a rundown of how things were going. He was pretty well exercised by the helicopter pilots—and you know Antonelli is probably the most listened-to officer in the outfit." I quickly caught myself. "Outside of you, of course."

The Major

It was true. Major Theodore Antonelli was not only the most revered officer, even the most cynical among us draftees viewed him as a model of what an officer should be, provided there had to be any such thing at all. Slight, solidly built, he had a boyish face made the more youthful by a hopping gait. He possessed a puckish intellect and a playfulness that was unbecoming an officer. And throughout the early stages, we marveled at his upscale serenity despite the many downs that beset the operation.

Word had circulated that in World War II, he had been awarded the Silver Star for outstanding bravery in the Italian campaign in 1945, and some regulars reported that he had been written up, actually in a comic book of combat feats. A comic book? Sure enough, a search turned up the magazine, and indeed it was replete with stories of men distinguished in battle. There was the young Antonelli, a wounded second lieutenant single-handedly fighting off an enemy counterattack.

There was no questioning Antonelli's shrewdness. Among the field grade officers, he was one of the few who mingled with us draftees, soliciting information and advice, and arguing about matters nonmilitary. Being in charge of the vital Research Division, Antonelli could be found everywhere, including the Three Ps where he would often plunk himself down on a bunk and shoot the bull about what was coming down and throw in what novel he was reading. His presence always offered surprises and his naturalness sparked many a free give-and-take discussion.

Nothing seemed to faze him, even when the joke was on him. Dropping by our tent one quiet evening, we offered him a can of beer. Dave opened it a bit too quickly. As he wrote to Mike, "I did a beautiful spray job all over his uniform." Antonelli howled. Dave was smitten. "He really is what I call a wonderful officer. I wish I worked for him."

At the same time, a certain peculiarity about him puzzled, and perturbed. It just didn't fit with our image of the perfect officer. Just outside the unit's perimeter Antonelli had the engineers level and smooth a portion of now partially softened tundra two by twenty feet. We couldn't figure what it was until there appeared a small, indented round cup at one end of the section. They had built a putting green, or to be more topographically accurate, a permafrost putting brown!

Every now and then Antonelli could be spotted practicing his game, muttering to himself as he sank or missed a putt, and occasionally walking around the compound with a golf club loping imaginary drives toward the fjord.

Late one afternoon in mid-operation he slipped into the Three Ps. As I recall, only Dave and I were working away at the time. He had no sooner eased himself onto a bunk than Dave, unable to contain himself, threw out the question many of us draftees had been raising over the many months: "Major, how come you're not in charge of this ramshackle operation?"

Antonelli smiled. "Made mistakes."

"You made mistakes!?" I exclaimed, stupidly.

"Yup, what's the matter, Boskin, you don't think I can make mistakes?"

I muttered some feeble reply—"Yeah but you're such a decorated soldier"—but wanted him to go on, "So, okay, what mistakes? Can we ask?"

He looked a bit thoughtful. "Sure, political ones. I was very brash and didn't cotton to the right people, in the right way, and at the right time."

"The right people? Meaning people like other mucky-muck officers?" asked Dave.

Antonelli peered at us, and chuckled.

Dave and I looked over at each other, silently wondering if we should continue. As it turned out, it wasn't a problem. Antonelli was his usual open, talkative self. "You guys aren't stupid. You've been in this quagmire long enough now to know how things work—though Boskin here can be an idiot when he takes on the colonel. Every operation, any type of operation anywhere, has a political component to it. What you have to do is figure out the type of situation you're in, the people you're involved with, and devise a strategy to get things done the way you want it done."

He drew in a breath, scrutinized what he was saying, and decided to go on.

"In the beginning I rarely took the political into account. Just did things the way I thought they should be done. And took some hits. Hell, I had a ball and didn't mind the consequences—again, in the beginning. Then as I got slightly older and wanted up the ladder, wanted more, I was kept down. So now I mind. That's why I volunteered for this operation. I'm using this for my next move."

"And here I thought," I cut into his monologue with some levity, "I was the only idiot who had volunteered for this godforsaken mission."

"Boskin—and you too, Van Dommelen"—he waved his hand at us, "may I say you guys aren't thick but maybe I should qualify that. Being dumb almost cost you both the recent promotion to corporal."

Promotion! None of us had had advance notice that we were up for it. An unexpected official communiqué from the C.O.'s office had informed us. Many of the draftees were moved up a notch, and we whooped. It meant added pay, something like ten dollars a month. We splurged! I immediately took off to the PX and purchased more film plus gifts for the three women on my letter-line. The booze blast that night kept us from moving too rapidly around the following day.

"Major, we didn't know a single thing about the promotions. What foolish stuff did we do?"

Antonelli leaned back on the bunk. "Anything cool in here to drink?"

Dave sheepishly handed him a cup of Kool-Aid. He tasted it, and grimaced. "Well, for starters, to get back to you, Boskin, there was that faux pas writing about the Helicopter Division and its refusal to move to Take-off Camp—and then informing the colonel that I had said it would cost the operation big if it remained here in Thule. Remember, big mouth . . . Stupid!"

With the word "stupid," I knew what was coming next. To protect and puff myself up before the C.O., I had betrayed him. I quickly tried to apologize. He waved me off. "Hey, I know why you told the C.O., and in my earlier days I probably would have done the same thing. But let me tell you something that you already know—another officer would have nailed your ass to the door and kept it perched there."

At that moment I realized several things, first that even though I was a draftee with no intention of an army career, this was his real world in the vastness of the military. So it was their "Spauldeen," as we used to say on my block, the coveted orange, high-bouncing ball that was the main item in our stick-ball games. The person who owns the ball makes up the rules, and since it was their ball, they also own the rules.

The second had to do with the meaning of the mission, and the so-called history. He really had me now. Yet what was this all about? Having already achieved an exalted position in our minds, he didn't need any additional mastery. Or did he? I could see he was grinning.

No more than a few seconds elapsed before the answer came. "Your ass aside," he said, "what matters here is the final history—but not necessarily yours."

I nodded a "go-on." Antonelli's grin disappeared. "You see, you think history is about revelation. Expose the past, or in this case the present, and things will be different in the future! Reveal the shortcomings and stupidities of this operation and the bigwigs in the Pentagon will rise up in wrath. They'll ensure it won't happen again. Not this way, ever again. Am I right?!"

I nodded more vigorously, yet knew enough to keep my mouth tightly shut.

"Wrong! They don't give a fucking hoot if it doesn't work. They'll try another tack if need be because they're convinced they've got the force of history on their side, the force of right against a powerful enemy, and one way or another we'll get the Russians." He was looking directly into my eyes.

But neither did he avoid Dave's. "There's always more money to fight the enemy. So your revelations don't amount to a hill of beans. What does count is the colonel's view, and mine, too. We want this thing to work, that's for sure, but if it doesn't," he paused for emphasis and spoke deliberately, "well then, we'll seemingly make it work. Got it!"

He then gave his full gaze to Dave. "And you, Van Dommelen, hah, you hide information from that monumental egotist Captain Lament because you know how off the wall he is. Now that's a real court-martial offense!"

Dave's ruddy face blanched whiter. "How'd you find that out?"

"Don't even ask! Don't matter! What does matter is that next time you come to me and we'll nail him to the colonel's door. Are you guys sure you have nothing better to drink than this sickening shit?"

So this was why he was sitting here, and complaining about our lousy Kool-Aid. Had he stopped at this point, our sense of him would have shifted.

But Antonelli wasn't through because for some reason or other he wanted to explain himself further. It was puzzling. Dave and I cut to each other's glance.

"In any case, I'm working on moving up and I've got a plan in action. Are you guys sure you haven't anything better to drink than—what the hell is this vile stuff? Kool-Aid?"

"Major," Dave replied, trying to save the day, "we have some great tea that my wife sent, could we brew you some? Also some great cookies my wife baked that survived the APO mail."

"No, thanks." Antonelli got up. "To repeat that line from Robert Frost, 'I've got miles to go before I sleep.'"

"Hold on, sir, if you don't mind," I exclaimed hurriedly, not wanting to push him too far but wanting to hear more. "A lot of us are really curious about your putting green and practicing golf swings. Are you getting ready for some golf tournament when we get back to the States?"

Hands on his hips, he stretched his upper body back and forth, and let out a yelp. "Yeah," he was grinning again, "in a way. You guys want to know why I'm into golf? All right, here's the deal. I've applied to the Army

War College. That's the place you have to go if you want up the ladder. John Eisenhower, the general's son, is there. And to these guys golf is serious business. If I want to get into their good graces I'd better be able to play a good game, which at present is pretty damn lousy. Any of you guys into golf?" We shook our heads. "Thought not. Catch you again—corporals!"

Crashes

All kinds of uncertainties beset the helicopters.

Problems arose from the violent swings in the weather with metal fatigue sapping their lives. Problems came from overworking the machines due to the constant requests. Then, for some inexplicable reasons, there were never enough available tools or replacement parts. Problems lay with the formula regulating flight-time. Pilots and mechanics counted on increasing their salary with overtime flights.

But with the unpredictable weather, only a few could fly beyond the allotted schedule. Fierce squabbles ensued, a situation naturally solved— has it ever been otherwise?—by RHIP: Rank Has Its Privileges. Only one minor shortcoming with this solution: the higher ranked were quite often the most inept.

Expectedly, as the mission wore on, fewer helicopters took to the air.

Despite these wrenching difficulties, we marveled that the birds were in the air at all, frequently when they shouldn't have been. At these times no salary could compensate them for the sheer number of hazards. They were flying fools.

So it came to pass one day that a helicopter crashed onto the ice cap, a mechanical failure. It was on a day that Major Theodore Antonelli was reviewing research teams and he was in the craft. He walked away. To rescue him came another helicopter. It flipped over as it took off, a pilot's error. Major Antonelli miraculously walked away a second time.

Later into the mission a third machine plummeted down. *Does it matter why?* Major Antonelli was in the craft at the time on an inspection trip. He was killed.

12

Top Secrets Away

Herr Captain Lament

Dave was beside himself. "I could say I am depressed," he wrote to his wife Mike in a letter on 30 June, "but actually I am just so mad that I could eat nails. If I had a canoe I would go AWOL."

Daynight after daynight, in a running commentary in his letters he lambasted the worsening situation. "The enlisted men are getting screwed every time they turn around. If they would just leave us alone we could do a good job here. They are so stupid with little things, that nothing is being accomplished."

He was ticked that the errors and inanities were being systematically purged from the status reports. "In all the historical reports that go to Washington, Joe tries to write the truth, but the colonel just lies and rewrites all the information so that *he* sounds good and that the operation is going well. If I had half a gut in me I would write Washington and tell them just what is going on up here."

What really got to him, though, were the security leaks in his own bailiwick. Despite his ceaseless efforts, he couldn't stem the seepage. "The security up here is horrible," he fumed, "every time I see what is going on I just about die. I feel it is my responsibility, yet there is nothing I can do to stop the spreading of important information. The enlisted men sit across from the civilians at chow and discuss classified information in front of them, and the officers assign people that do not have security clearance to jobs that require SECRET clearances. I have tried my best, but can see that it does no good."

To Dave, and others as well, Captain Phillip Lament, chief of intelligence, was the primary culprit in the breakdown of security. Dave recorded it in his letters every step of the way, his disaffection beginning early on in the operation.

"We have no materials to work with. All the things Capt. Lament had me bring up here are just plain stupid. We wasted all kinds of space on manuals and books that will never be opened, and left wonderful office supplies back in the States." Dave was specifically referring to such instructional works as *Drill and Ceremonies* that Lament had ordered. One of the helicopter mechanics spotted the manual and blew his top. "Why couldn't he have shipped up tool sets so we could repair the 'copters?" he shouted. "Who the hell is going to read these stupid manuals, anyway?" Dave shrugged his shoulders in helplessness.

Nightday after nightday, he scribbled furiously to Mike venting his ascending spleen. Lament took off to tour Nuna Takeoff Camp. "Capt. Lament has left us again. Before he departed he gently told us we were evicted from our Atwell. This, of course, made us all extremely unhappy. Major Antonelli arrived at our little abode and after a cry on his shoulders he gave us permission to remain here. In a few words he told Lament to go to hell."

Dave shuddered at his return. "Captain Lament is due back soon. I do not think his welcome will be very good. He seems to have made many enemies since his arrival here—and I cannot say that I blame those people."

Once back in the compound, Lament ordered his chicken-shit changes. "The whole place is going ape. Capt. Lament decides we should spend five minutes a day policing up the area." We were to put it mildly, ripshit!

He didn't always succeed, though. "Lament pulled a real shrewdy today, but it backfired on the ol' boy. It went like this: He noticed that one of Major Antonelli's boys was wearing his pants unbloused and told him to blouse them. Well, the major saw Steve and me with unbloused pants. He told us to come over to his desk. We, of course, knew what his plan was. He had us stand in front of Lament and said, 'You had better clean your own backyard before cleaning someone else's.' Lament was roaring mad, but what could he say? So of course we had to blouse our pants into our boots, but we enjoyed doing that after we had seen Lament crawl into his hole."

Yet he also managed to outmaneuver Antonelli and it was because of his outstretch for power that we were removed from our Atwell and shifted into a tent that immediately caused enormous administrative bottlenecks. "As you can see by the address we have moved again," Dave explained to his wife. "Dear Capt. Phillip Boy generously donated our Atwell to headquarters as a briefing room for VIPs. He certainly is a jerk— to say the least. He is one man who will not stand behind his men at all. He has been keeping his face well hidden from us since we got the notice. We did not have a place to go. We hunted around, the five of us plus junior scientists, and finally ended up in a tent."

But the problem went far beyond Lament's compulsive power maneuvers, minute or grandiose. It went to the heart of protecting the mission itself, and whether the resulting history would offer insight into its problematic outcome for future missions.

"I feel my whole job here has been lost in the great crevasses of the Greenland Ice Cap," Dave wrote immediately after another disturbing episode. "Just today Capt. Lament gave Joe a map that was loaded with secret information and Joe thought it should have at least a secret classification. He brought it to me to see what I thought. Well naturally I thought it should be classified, but Capt. Lament said no. What can one do when he is overpowered by an idiot? He even said it was classified information, but would not let me classify it. Actually, I don't give a god-damn if all this gets into the hands of the Russians or not because I will not be up here next year."

At night we certainly cursed aloud in the Three Ps, and wondered whether it would ever be possible to halt the man, plug the sieve, finesse the situation. "That *miserablebastard*," Dave constantly muttered, "I hope the I.G. (inspector general) finds the things he has not been doing in his job." As it turned out, we didn't have long to wait. Hubris, that wonderful human frailty, came to our rescue, as it so often does in history.

Belittling Themiserablebastard

"That's it," whooped Dave.
   "What's it?"

"The way to get rid of him."

"The way to get rid of who? Lament, you mean?!"

"Sure, him! Who else but that *miserablebastard*!"

"Seems this has become one of your favorite phrases. Why not call him a schmuck?"

"You know I don't usually use that word—but, yeah, he's sure that."

"Okay, I'll bite, how do you propose to get rid of him?"

"Well, maybe not get rid of—but humiliate the schmuck!"

"I see you've given it much thought lately."

"You know I'm always thinking about it! The *miserablebastard* consumes me. He just about undermines everything he gets his fingers into—and he's into everything. He is such a fucking menace."

"Okay, then, how do you propose to humiliate him?"

"Guess, what? General Sherman Tiller of the I.G.'s Office is coming to Thule this week, can you believe it! Lament, Antonelli and myself, with a few other enlisted men, had a conference to decide how we shall hoodwink the dear man and his staff. From Lament's little talk he carefully told us—in a tactful manner, of course—that he didn't want us to give out any facts that would put him in a bad spot. Boy, I thought, what I could do to this joint if I wanted to! Then I said to myself, why the hell not!? Go for it, go for the artistic gold."

Hustling the Big General

Preparing for General Tiller's visit, Lament spared no one and ignored all other tasks. The man wanted his promotion to the hallowed field grade officer of major and needed the general's highest recommendation. He had planned to snow him . . . in Greenland.

In his new Atwell headquarters that was once our offices, Lament ordered buddy Bill Stromp to construct special shelving and cases that would show off the gravity of his section. A draftee from Detroit, Bill was a whiz carpenter, except on those occasions when he was slightly depressed being so far removed from his wife, and hugged the bottle too much and got his dimensions slightly off. Once, early in the operation, he built an impressive and stylish complex of shelves and closets for the C.O. Overly awed by the colonel's girth and command, though, he oversized them. It took half a dozen men many hours to get the sections through the door, and even then he had to rebuild some of it.

Bill, though, loved a construction challenge, and eagerly dove into Lament's project. Only a single obstacle stood in the way. Most of the high-grade lumber had been consumed in Thule's construction and wood was scarce. To scrounge discarded pieces at the huge base dump was out of the question to Lament. On his own authority, he sent through a special requisition on the grounds that General Tiller's visit had the "highest national security priority."

"Can you believe what he's doing?" yelled Dave to a group playing Battleship. Not waiting for a reply, his voice rose a notch; Dave wanted attention. "That *miserablebastard*, he's having Bill build top-quality shelves and cases for him!"

Steve looked up. "What's this all about, Pogo?" Steve had a knack for nicknames—mine was Mandrake the Magician.

Knowing what was coming down the pike, I groaned so all could hear. "Next week General Sherman Tiller, the chief of intelligence, is coming for a site visit. Lament wants to impress him. He's up for promotion to major."

"That *miserablebastard*," repeated Dave, almost always mild mannered, "he doesn't do shit, gets everything wrong, tries to take over other sections, makes a mess of security, he's a mass of egotism. Ask Joe, he's the only officer who actually likes writing the status reports because he blows his accomplishments way out of proportion. And now he's even got Joe doing work on intelligence files at night!"

All of which was true, including having been ordered by him to assist in his work after my status reports were filed.

Everyone nodded as if to say so what else is new! and went back to Battleship. As usual it ended in a rout as the geologists sank us pencil pushers.

Dave grabbed a book from the tent library and retreated to his bunk. I plunked down and opened a magazine. Dave peered over and whispered conspiratorially, "Hey, Joe, I think I've devised a plan to get even—but I need your help." My eyes did an involuntary roll upward.

To my surprise, it turned out to be as easy as a lament.

Nothing Quite like Humiliation . . .

Phillip Lament prized his seemingly photographic mind. He went around claiming he never met a document he didn't like, always remembered who sent it, which file drawer it was in, who had copies of it, and on and on. He constantly reminded one and all that he was a whiz of an administrator, clearly destined for higher things. "And that," exclaimed Dave with a wry smile, "will prove his undoing."

The next day he sprang his strategy on the Three Ps, and he was like a teenager about to get his first driving lesson. His artistic hands weaving designs in the air, Dave eagerly spelled out his strategy, a plan that possessed the splendor of simplicity and the consternation of a crevasse. "Listen, all we have to do is move some files around, mix others up, and maybe even lose a couple. Then when it comes time for him to produce a specific item, to show them to the general, they won't be there. Simple as that."

"Is that *all* we have to do?" I asked sarcastically.

"Yeah," Dave countered, "Yeah, I know what you're alluding to, but it's doable. I know because that *miserablebastard* doesn't have the photographic mind he claims he does."

We all knew Dave was agitated because his arms were flying around. "The one person who knows where the files are—is me! Really! He relies on me to produce 'em. He's always asking me where something or other is. My problem here is how to snooker him without fingering me as the culprit."

"Is that all, Pogo?" said Steve skeptically. "Hey, great plan, Kemosabe!"

"Steve, for god's sake, we can do it. Let me show you how."

Steve had invoked the closing line of an old Lone Ranger–Tonto joke: The masked man and his side-kick Tonto, whom he referred to as "Kemosabe," are surrounded by a group of hostile Indians. The Lone Ranger orders an attack by the two of them. "Who's we, Kemosabe!?" replies Tonto. So whenever some dubious scheme involving that personal pronoun elevated up, the response was always, "Who's we, Kemosabe!?"

Buddy Dave was up to the challenge, and scenarioed what appeared to be a simple game plan. Who would have suspected the artist as spy? Little did I know then what he revealed many decades later. In any case, Dave would have top-secret files winding up in the C.O.'s filing cabinet, misplaced in Lament's own system, or just plain gone.

"Missing?" I asked dubiously, "how do files wind up simply missing? Gone?? Someone's going to suggest they've been stolen, and that would get a search going. They'd be frantic that there was this spy among us. If not some spy, then the CID [Criminal Investigation Division] plant, whoever he is, would come into play here. Then the guy who had swiped them would be charged for a major security breach, and hell, Dave, that's your own bailiwick."

That struck a chord. "Yeah, CID agent, what about that, Pogo?" Steve piped up.

Every top-secret company had a Pentagon undercover plant from the Criminal Investigation Division whose purpose was to root out possible criminal activity, or worse, this being the 1950s, a subversive activity in particular. Without doubt the CID agent was in a top-top-secret class of his own, meaning that no one knew who he was, including the C.O. Dave and I mused about his identity throughout the mission and each time a different person headed up the list. We never did agree about who it was and eventually gave up trying. Never did I suspect . . .

Dave was adamant. "Yep, missing files. If there is a search for a spy, I'll show that every man in this outfit has gone through plenty of security checks. This is my job, after all. Nope, no spies will be found because there aren't any—but there will be doubts about Lament himself because of all the other snafus that will suddenly show up."

"Now hold on a minute, Dave," I countered. Just then Tom came into the tent. His entrances, like his exits, were always serene, like television's Mr. Rogers or Mr. Peepers. We were so into our conversation that we barely noticed him. He sat down on the edge of his bunk, removed his boots and carefully placed them side by side next to his footlocker, the only pair standing at attention in the tent.

"Okay," he said in his reedy, churchy voice, "what're you guys whispering about? Who're you bitching about this time? Not me I hope."

We fell silent. Tom was the C.O.'s right-hand man, and although he was ramrod straight there was slight apprehension that he might inadvertently say something to him. Tom stretched out on his bed, looked upward and softly whispered, "Okay, if you won't tell me, I won't ever tell you again either."

We cracked up. Always surprising, always playing against type. Just a few days earlier Steve and I entered to find Tom doing push-ups, a practice he regularly did in late afternoons before chow. It was a calm day and warm in the tent and Tom was wearing a white t-shirt and briefs. Not saying anything, we watched as he cadence counted. I don't know why we watched, nothing else to distract I suppose. Then Tom slowed down, and it was clear that he was self-conscious. Keeping his head pointed to the floor, he said in anguish, "God, is my dick showing!?" "Tom," exclaimed Steve impishly, "is that upper or lower case?"

In hushed tones, the conversation picked up again. Dave repeated his plot. Now Tom was enlisted in the scheme. His proximity to the C.O. put him in a perfect position to move files around the office.

Despite Dave's assurance, though, the problem of "files missing" was a large hurdle. Tom was up to it. "Didn't you tell me a couple of weeks ago that Lament gave Joe some top-secret manuscripts without classifying them? And didn't Lament also think it wasn't even necessary to classify them, against regulations! Well, what happened to them? They're your missing files! Put them somewhere no one can find them until just before we leave here."

"Wonderful," I declared, "problem solved."

"Where are they now?" asked Tom.

I looked over at Dave who looked back at me. Neither of us could remember what we did with them. "Fuck," I exclaimed as we racked our brains, "here we are trying to do in Lament when we don't even know what we did with the damned files ourselves!"

"Backtrack," said Tom the altar boy, calmly, "go back and take it step by step."

Dave quickly found them. He had put them into his own secret cache for keeping just in case the Inspector General ever decided to investigate TRARG.

Routing Themiserablebastard

Spiffy. All was spiffy when General Sherman Tiller, his two stars radiating out from a starched cap, arrived at the compound. A week before the outfit had delivered fatigues to the Air Post's dry cleaners with strict instructions that they be ready for the general's visit. All of us tried hard to stand soldierly in front of our Atwells and tents as he rode by in a jeep. We were woefully out of synch, shifting our feet and scratching ourselves.

The colonel and the general smiled at each other as they briskly saluted. After an hour or so they emerged from the C.O.'s plush Atwell quarters, broad smiles on their faces, heads prancing from imbibing first-rate scotch, and began their inspection of the operation.

Four minutes, maybe, consumed the inspection. Their visit at my desk couldn't have lasted more than that. What I do recall is having taken down my sign, HYSTORICAL DIVISION, and replaced it with the correct spelling. The C.O. introduced me. He was proud, he said beamingly, "to have in his outfit a professional historian."

The general smiled and said I was the first noncom he had met in this position and that he personally liked history enormously in college. "I'm a Civil War buff myself," he said animatedly. "I belong to an organization which meets every year. Do you know it?" I didn't, but there was no sense in appearing ignorant, so I nodded that it sounded familiar. "What kind of historian are you?" he wanted to know. To my reply that I've concentrated on social history and planned to get a Ph.D. after my stint, he shook his head approvingly. "Good, that's very good. Keep in touch." I told him I would "Sir."

Then, as he was about to move on, he shot a question. "So, Colonel Balstrum tells me you're going to write a history of *this* mission? Well, Corporal, make it a full one—I want to read all about the amazing accomplishments of this outfit. Don't leave anything out." Before I could reply, the colonel took his arm and led him out of the tent as we all saluted. Steve looked at me and winked, softly mouthing some Shakespearean lines like Mandrake the Magician. There was not going to be another question about the history.

Briskly darting in and out of Atwells, all went smoothly until the entourage went into the Intelligence Division's office that Captain Lament had sleeked up for the general's visit. Present were Lament and several other officers, including Major Antonelli, and Dave himself. The stay lasted almost thirty minutes. To Lament, however, it seemed like too many hours.

Unlike his desultory interest in the mission history, the general demanded the specifics of intelligence findings. He especially wanted the maps of crevasse locations and data on the performance of snow vehicles and helicopters, and he wanted to know if every military man and civilian scientist had been cleared for top-secret materials.

Lament was ever-efficient, laying out the files on his brand-new massive desk. Then came a glitch. Lament snapped open up a file drawer, slid his fingers across the manila tabs searching for information on the crucial Snow Cat tracked vehicles and similar transports, and looked puzzled. He went back to the beginning, moving his fingers across the folders with increased speed. Imperceptibly mumbling to himself "they're here, I know they're here," he quickly scrutinized the label on the file drawer. Eyes scrunched, he looked over at Dave who didn't blink an eye. Finally, he turned back to the General. "Sir, they seem to have been misplaced. I'll get them to you before you depart, General."

"Captain, where might they be??" The C.O. was obviously displeased.

"I don't know, sir," replied a plaintive Lament.

"Let's proceed, shall we," declared the General. "I would like to see the files on the French scientists. Was it difficult getting information on them?"

"Well, sir, it took some time but all's correct with them."

"What about the English boys? We're especially concerned about them."

Lament stared at the general, trying to remember them. Something stirred in his mind but it didn't register. And stared some more. For the life of him he couldn't recall because those were the documents he had given to me for some inexplicable reason and I had turned them over to Dave! Lament frantically sought help. "Van Dommelen," he said, "do you know where we have those particular dossiers?"

"No sir," replied Dave as straightforward as possible, "it should be in the section on civilian scientists, which you personally handled." Dave could barely contain himself.

"Right," exclaimed Lament, "then that's where they will be." Opening the metal cabinet, he rummaged through the folders—and found nothing.

He quickly went through it again. "Where??" he muttered. "They seem to be misplaced." Realizing he had just made a terrible mistake, Lament swiftly blurted out, "Just for the moment! I'll get them to you as soon as possible, General."

"Files missing!?" said the C.O. incredulously. "That's not possible, Captain. Nor is it acceptable. You better find them pronto, you understand me, Lament!!" Shaken, Lament managed to make it through the next ten minutes, producing whatever else the general had asked for. The damage had been done, though, and after the general and colonel departed he began a frantic search for the documents.

Dave, Tom, and I ransacked his office and sorrowfully came up empty-handed. Figuring that he could score some future points, Dave guessed where they might have gone. Sure enough, Lament found them. He scooted out.

But to Lament's further embarrassment, the data on the Snow Cat vehicles were located in the C.O.'s office where Tom had surreptitiously placed them. To our own consternation, though, the folders on the English scientists had simply vanished. Unless Dave still retains them in some hidden place, they are lost to history.

As for Lament's promotion, he left our outfit soon after TRARG returned to Fort Eustis and we never did find out whether he made it or not. By that time it didn't matter. What did matter in the Three Ps was the phrase *miserablebastard* never again being uttered from Dave's lips. It was a welcome relief.

13

Never a Dull Tent

The Famishes

Bitching and eating—or was it the other way around?—uplifted, nourished, comically propelled us.

When we worked, we bitched and ate; when we weren't working, we ate and bitched; when we played Battleship or poker, we bitched and ate; when we got into lengthy discussions, we ate and bitched. There was never a time we didn't do both. Then, when a purloined stash of beer or bottle suddenly materialized, both the bitching and eating got sloshed away.

The tent was always filled with food. Not fast food but tidbit-food. Because we were constantly famished—a situation that had nothing to do with being hungry—ongoing nourishment was imperative. The cravings sprang from the entangling exigencies of ceaseless work, endless frustration, and collateral damage to our sex lives.

Munchies magically surfaced in our tent, brought by Three Wise Men seeking the Messiah who somehow got lost and wound up in the Arctic. It's not only in the desert where such apparitions conjure solace. At times, Mess Gadget slid in to offer up his latest tidbit experiments, which went along with his "shooting the shit."

And some items we actually purchased via the thriving "snow market," Thule's counterpart to the black market version that operated around the clock. Hard cash actions ran contrary to protocol; in the military trafficking is the big trade. Everyone in every branch of service is perpetually on the swap prowl.

Our Three Ps tent was not just on the river of exchange, we were docked at the major port. Trading favors with the air force and the navy, hustling the civilians, Inuits, and officers, hell, we would have bargained with the Enemy if they had been around. In exchange for banana bread came pure water from the air force's photo lab; in exchange for girlie magazines came pure coffee from Gadget's dining supply; in exchange for pulp fiction came pure eggs from the navy; in exchange for ghost-writing love letters came pure ceramic cups from Rich's endless depot.

What we couldn't barter, we borrowed. What we couldn't borrow, we pilfered. A caravan of large, arctic parkas and fur hats moved stealthily along the tundra streets, treading through and around the vast base, peering into its cubbyholes and hustling off with silverware, napkins, rolls, butter, desserts, salt and pepper shakers, pots, pans, toilet paper—anything that wasn't nailed down. We dubbed our parkas "Harpos," after the Marx Brother's comic coat that always tumbled out purloined items.

When Dave did some special typing for the air force's provisions branch, he scrounged cartons of canned milk and cocoa. Colorful ribbons rafted down from our tent's roof, a gift from the base tailor shop after Tom had gone there to pick up the C.O.'s uniform. A long wooden bench strangely wound up in the middle of the floor, which by this time had taken on the appearance of a rural roadhouse.

Another miracle came from post office heaven. A flow of packages wound up in the tent. Dave was especially bombarded with an assortment of goodies from his embracing wife Mike, plus his parents. I was envious. His was the first to arrive after we had deplaned and it brought hooplas from the guys sitting around. Dave always tore into it. A luscious spread of candy lined the top, and underneath were slender packets that brought howls: Kool-Aid! "It was very comical," Dave playfully admonished Mike, "what the hell am I going to do with Kool-Aid? Maybe on the 4th of July we can invent some drink along with a bottle of something."

But nobody wanted to wait for the Fourth! Later that night the packets were retrieved. And instantly an argument ensued over how to savor its contents: what, exactly, would be the best ingredient to "flavor" the "flavor" with?? Before this question could be answered, there was the immediate problem of a receptacle. So we cleaned out the communal coffeepot as best we could, poured in a couple of packets, and using a geological ruler, stirred furiously. Slowly an icky brownish lime coloration emerged. It didn't faze anyone. Into the pot went the gin.

The pot was passed around. Coffee cups filled up and Dave proposed a toast to the *Guinness Book of World Records*. "We are the first," he said delightedly, "to make Kool-Aid north of the Arctic Circle!" Yeas resounded.

It was awful, tasting like diluted lime Jello and bog water. Gagging, Steve let out a cry that only comes from someone who has been side-blinded on the football field. "Pogo," he said pointing to Dave with his earliest nickname, "this is the worst shit I've tasted since I was a twelve year old in my small town in Michigan." Who knows why the affectionate name of the comic strip had popped into Steve's head? "Pogo, you have added meaning to the mighty Bard who wrote, "'The purest spring is not so free from mud,' *Henry VI*, Part 2."

No one disputed him. "It needs a powerful antidote," Steve declared. "I suggest more gin." "There is no more gin," I said, "that was the last of the barrel." Steve grinned, the smirk of an urchin. "Unless someone's found my stash . . ." He went over to his bunk. "Now, before I haul it out, much as I love but don't trust any of you bastards, I mean everyone of you, turn around and no one so much as peeks until I say so."

When eyes opened, there stood a beaming Steve, his ornate flask held aloft. More gin quickly gushed in, and cups filled up again. The Kool-Aid was now completely overcome and only a whiff of coffee beans remained. Steve proposed his Shakespearean toast: "Act II, Scene III, *As You Like It:* 'I would give all my fame for a pot of ale and safety.'" Yeas abounded. This only encouraged Steve once more. "Gentlemen," he turned in a complete circle, "may I add another from the almighty Bard, though I'm a bit too crocked to remember where . . ."

Even though he was straddling his footlocker, it looked as if he was about to topple over any second. But he gamely carried on: "Muster your wits: stand in your own defense; Or hide your heads like cowards, and fly hence."

"Steve," said Tom, shaking his head, "what the hell does that have to do with this swill??"

"Nothing," replied Steve, smirking, "nothing at all. I just like the ring of it."

10. "Your turn, Dave, tell me again what the fuck we're doing up here?"

Envy Envelops

I was envious! Hell, we were all envious!

Dave was deluged with packages. Five arrived on a single day. All sorts of goodies, like fudge, breads and cookies, and despite Dave's droll asides, more Kool-Aid. It was agreed, he was the Three Ps Grand Receiver = TRARG's TPGR.

All of us were covetous, which instantly prompted Tom, Steve, and I to compose beseeching letters for home treats. I knew exactly what I wanted. A close friend of my father's, Warshay, owned arguably the best delicatessen in Brighton Beach, at least that was the boast to which my father wholeheartedly subscribed. They exchanged favors for one another, my father did his plumbing and carried home corned beef and brisket.

Exhorting him to send Warshay's best salamis, I also asked for chocolate marshmallow cookies, my favorite. I said nothing about Kool-Aid.

We all mailed our requests on the same day and, amazingly, three weeks later an assortment of packages arrived precisely at the identical time. Happily, none was for Dave, a vindication of sorts.

I got to go first and ripped open the box. No sooner had the paper come off than we all knew something was amiss. A horrible odor buffeted the tent. "Uh oh," said Steve, "I suspect foul play." Tearing open the inside wrapping, I saw a fat, shrunken, green-and-white-flecked salami. "Ghastly," Dave wrote to Mike, "it reminded me of a large mouse under a box."

"Even Mandrake the Magician, hell, not even Houdini, can turn this salami back to its original uncircumcised form," said Steve.

Tom opened his next. Inside was a cake in relatively good shape but the frosting had turned black. He looked terribly disappointed. "Tom, I don't think that's how it was sent," said Dave soothingly.

Steve waited for last. His eyes peering upward as he gently opened up his box, he let out a sigh. "Ah, just what the man asked for! Jars of olives, cans of nuts, a metal stirrer, and hey, Michigan cookies!" He was jubilant. "Gentlemen, all we need is some more of the C.O.'s magnificent, first-class gin!"

We laughed, then caught ourselves. "What did you say?" a voice popped up. "Are you for real?" asked Tom, his mouth wide open. Dave looked on bemusedly. It was a good thing our gentle but stern regular sergeants, Cupps and Sexton, were out of the tent.

Steve hummed some jolly tune.

"Cut it out," Dave whispered quizzically, "what've you been up to? Are you totally crazy?"

Steve looked cherubic. "Oh, guys," he said evenly, "don't get your balls in an uproar. Nothing's going to happen."

Tom's voice was shaky. He was vulnerable because he had the keys and combinations to the C.O.'s office. "Steve," he said pleadingly, "say you're kidding! You're kidding, right!?"

"Right," we all chorused, "say it!" Panicky eyes peered in on Steve who was opening the jar and can.

"Hey, c'mon, guys, loosen up. None of you have anything to get excited about, except that more gin is definitely needed and," he added with a sardonic twist, "required to fulfill our lofty mission. Nobody's going to get into trouble . . . Here's how I did it . . ."

Everyone groaned in unison.

"You know those huge boxes that come to the C.O.'s Atwell on a weekly basis—weekly, mind you." He pointed at me. "Well, Joe, you ought to know because you cart 'em in whenever they need an extra hand."

Large shipments to the compound invariably produced a familiar order from the supply sergeant: "Fuck the history, Boskin, haul in the C.O.'s crates." I dropped whatever I was doing and hustled over to the Supply Atwell, a couple of hundred yards away.

Because the crates went directly into the colonel's office, I assumed they contained top-secret scientific directives or apparatus. At the outset, I knew next to nothing about the technological end of the operation and so postulated that items like sensitive crevasse detectors and electronic gear were in the various crates. The boxes ran from the compact to hefty sizes.

I had forgotten the admonition of a particular insightful sociology professor in undergraduate school who whiplashed us with his favorite maxim: "Never—no never-ever—trust your assumptions and always but-always question them."

"You really mean to say you haven't the vaguest idea what's in those crates?" asked Steve, a trifle skeptically.

"Honestly, Steve, I haven't the inklingest. I assume they're top secret scientific equipment of sorts. But I get the feeling that you're telling me otherwise."

Steve sighed, his eyes moving up the tent wall, "Mostly gallon bottles of booze—and I mean gallon bottles!"

"Gallons of what?" I exclaimed. "I've never seen such a thing." Palms up, I turned to Dave and Tom, "Have you guys??" Heads shook. "Jesus," said Steve, a finger wagging at us, "you guys are pitiful. I'm back in fuck-ing kindergarten."

Reining in my stupidity, I was still dubious. "You're saying that in those huge crates that I lug into the C.O.'s Atwell every week are bottles of booze—just that!?"

"Nope, there is some stuff from the Pentagon but . . ." he paused for a quiet laugh, "otherwise, hey, not ordinary bottles, duncehead. Gallon jugs of the best scotch, bourbon, and gin. Mostly scotch and bourbon, though. So it's easy for me to skip over when I know the place's empty and fill up my little flask. There's always, yep always, half-full bottles. The C.O. never misses it. He never keeps tab."

"But those boxes have been coming in regularly," I declared incredulously. "Are you telling us that the brass consumes that much booze??" It was so far removed from my own bailiwick of Brighton Beach where my first drink was a mixture of rye and ginger. I was seventeen. Two drinks produced bliss and more meant slumber. College was wine coolers and beer because I couldn't afford anything else.

Steve shook his head in admiration. "Yeah, the brass boozes it up almost every night and they've got lots of company. Every goddamn congressman and Pentagon flunky who comes up here is treated to a royal welcome. Good booze hides an awful lot of shit. If you guys don't know that, well, it's time you got with it."

"How do you manage to get into his Atwell without being detected?" Dave asked, somewhat skeptical.

"Pogo and Mandrake, two peas in a dumb pod . . . I get in because the C.O. asks me to." Steve grinned like a Cheshire cat.

"I don't believe it," said Tom, "no freaking way." Even this late into the operation, he still couldn't bring himself to say "fuck."

Not Steve, of course. "Who the fuck do you think cleans up the mess after they have one of their rollicking drinking times? Me! 'Cause I am the lowest of the lowly—and what's more there's nothing more lowly than being the lowliest." His laugh rumbled up the sides of the tent.

"Got a Shakespearean line for our ignorance?" Tom's inquiry had a half-derisive pitch to it.

"Sure I do—but you guys aren't worth one. Now, for fuck's sake let's get on with the drinking!"

Real Eggs

Some items, though, were hard to get. These challenges led to special strategizing sessions. Pirating expeditions in search of truly elusive delicacies became the highest priority.

Like real eggs.

Within a month after arriving we had developed a Pavlovian loathing for the starchy, gooey, powdered eggs that were served up in the air force noncom mess halls. It had the taste and nutritional value of barroom sawdust.

After returning from another meal of powdered eggs, geologist Don offered a whimsically persuasive narrative that the US Geological Survey—for obvious reasons, the agency had several civilian scientists attached to the outfit—had recently discovered strata of powdered-egg pools thousands of feet beneath the ice cap. Fellow geologists stationed at the Pentagon had conspiratorially informed him of a top-secret memo ordering powdered eggs to pipe into noncom mess halls in Thule. Only the officers were allowed real eggs. After a short discussion, our clique of draftees agreed that if Moscow Molly and Leningrad Lenny were really smart, they would denounce powdered eggs as the worst form of capitalist degeneration.

Real eggs remained exasperatingly elusive. The deprivation factor soared. Delusions of omelets and sunny-side ups swept through the tent.

My reputation as historian soared the very day I brought back eleven fresh eggs. It had nothing to do with history itself.

I had just completed a stint of K.P. at the Thule officers mess hall and was getting my gear at the rear entrance when I spotted crates of unloaded food. I hung around pretending to search for a lost glove, then quietly made my way around the stacked boxes stenciled with fruit and vegetables and suddenly there it was: EGGS.

With only a couple of air force stevedores working, I waited until they were out of sight. Swooping down, I ripped open a box. There were rows and rows of white eggs. Sons-of-bitches officers! Gingerly placing several in each of my parka upper and lower side pockets, I sidled away. Then I got greedy and swooped down for more.

Departing nonchalantly, I prayed. It was not about getting caught, rather about not squashing the eggs as I maneuvered along the rocky, tundra roads, offering up a special ode to the Ice Gods not to send down a whiteout.

"EGGS, EGGS!" I shouted like an idiot as I entered the Three Ps. Within seconds I was surrounded. The eggs were stashed away for an evening feast.

After remaining hidden for a couple of days in Dave's Top Secret filing drawer, an invite went out to a selective bunch. There were not enough to go around for a special style so a decision was made to boil them. Placing them into a metal pot supplied by Gadget, the tent stove was hiked up.

All eyes focused on the pot. An interminable time elapsed while we waited for the water to boil. It was going too slowly. "Take one out," exclaimed Gil, the gentle geologist who rarely raised his voice, but impatient like the rest of us, "let's test it." A spoon reached in, retrieved an egg, and was handed over to Gil. The egg was steaming hot. "Ay!" he yelped as he juggled the egg between his hands, and hurriedly threw it to someone next to him. The guy also found it sizzling and shifted it to the next one. The egg wound up in the hands of Herb, a botanist with a flower soul—and suddenly it exploded, covering his shirt and face. It was only half-cooked and smelled terrible.

The place went hysterical.

"Joe," said Steve in down-toned sarcasm, "do us a favor and don't steal any more eggs. Your history might be good, but you are positively the worst crook."

"Oh, c'mon, this isn't Joe's fault," said buddy Dave, coming to my rescue. "We just didn't let the eggs boil long enough. Give it time."

We all agreed they were the best eggs we had ever tasted. I secretly gave Dave half of mine.

Tent Songs

Geologists are a strange breed. The lowly ground is their hallowed bailiwick, the offer of true revelation. They're into rocks and more rocks. On their minds, squirreled in their pockets, magnified under glass, filed and categorized along historical zones, their focus is down while they pray up, hoping to discover clues to whatever they are seeking. Traveling singly or in packs, their bodies ritualize as they stoop, chip, probe, jotting slowly into small, black notebooks, size, location, type of rock, their emotions as expressive as the rocks themselves.

So, too, as Dave and I soon discovered, were their politics. When not battling the geologists in a game of Battleship, we battled them in a game of corporate oil politics. The oil companies ruined where they probed, we argued; it was for the good of all, they replied. The oil depletion allowance particularly rankled, a special privilege, we contended; the geologists defended it as a venture risk in which the companies often lost. The oil interests forged alliance with the most repressive regimes around the world, we fumed; that was beyond the purview of the oil companies, an internal affair, they countered. The earth belongs to the people, we howled; the oil companies had a God-given, Adam Smith, right to explore, they smiled.

Cautious in politics, they were anything but in their songs, songs they had picked up from fellow geologists on rocky slopes all over the earth. Their range of bawdy songs always dazzled, and spurred us on. At least most of us. After numerous trips to the outlying fields, Don would saunter in the Three Ps with his small ukulele and begin the festivities. Strumming familiar camp songs at first, he would then launch into bawdy, obscene songs that were uproarious.

At the first hint of their venue, though, straight-laced Tom would cup hands over ears, admonish about blasphemy, and depart the tent. Later, when the geologists were gone, he would reproach Dave and me. "How could you," he said half-deploring, half-angrily, "sing those songs?! You guys are so concerned about people's feelings, and you talk all the time about injustice, and then you sing those vile words."

No valid history of TRARG should go down without at least one well-known risqué ballad, one that truly rattled Tom. Of a World War I, English vintage, *I Don't Want to Join the Army* should be attended by a Cockney accent, at least a smidgen of the words and inflection recalled over half-century ago:

Chorus

Oh I don't want to join the army,
I don't want to go to war,
I just want to hang around the Piccadilly Underground
And live off the earnings of a high-clad lady;

Don't want a bayonet up my arse hole,
Don't want my bollocks shot away,
I just want to live in England
Jolly, jolly England
And fornicate me fuckin' life away;

Verse

Monday night I touched her on the ankle
Tuesday night I touched her on her knee
Wednesday night with some success I lifted her bloomin'
    dress
Thursday night what I did see
Friday night I put my hands upon it
Saturday night she gave my balls a tweak
But it was Sunday after supper that I shoved the old boy
    upp-er,
And now I'm paying thirty-bob a week . . .

11. Last beer before the fire.

Oh I don't want to join the army,
I don't want to go to war . . .

Disinherit the Wind

It was 20 July, the height of summer, and the storm was fierce. Dave yelled out it was a 2.4 phase storm and I had no reason to contest his figures, though I had no idea what he was talking about. He must have picked that one up from an intelligence report, his curiosity being boundless, or better, from one of the geologists.

The day before had been lovely, a genial breeze wafting off the fjord and temperatures hovering in the high 20s, the vast sky an entertaining cobalt blue. Then, as is often the case in the Arctic, a sudden, sullen wind whipped in and the cerulean grimly disappeared. An unwelcome caller, a mini-whiteout, washed away everything visible. The only sound was a nasty cry from the swirling gusts.

Intensifying during the day, the wind upended loose boards and rocks, hurtling them against the tent. We were forced outside to pick up the debris to prevent them from slicing through the canvas. The tent flaps were swinging like elephant ears.

Dave got into a poetic state. "The tent is moving back and forth like a ballet dancer," he sang out. Always the artist, I thought. "More like Martha Graham dancers," I insisted, remembering the undergraduate time when I assisted setting up the staging for her troupe in exchange for watching them perform at the college.

Inside, everything was in a warm state of disarray. Papers and books were strewn on the footlockers, empty juice cans and cooking pans littered the floor, a canister of Kool-Aid with cups and cookies adorned the bench. Both potbellied stoves were fired up as high as possible.

"Time for some inner warmth," declared Sexton as he swigged luke-cold beer. Cupps joined him. Steve pulled out his flask. He offered it up. Dave, Tom, and I shook our heads. "Actually, I would prefer some hot chocolate," said Tom, pouring some water into a pot. "Add for me," I said. "Me, too," piped in Dave. Now that, I thought, was true camaraderie, half the tent hard-nose guzzlers, half sweet-tooth nourishers.

Everyone was singularly occupied. The fierce wind had closed down all talk. The tent continued its tug-of-war dance with the wind, the guide ropes straining against the rock-filled barrels, but no big deal. At some point or other the last light was turned off. The tent turned dark. We hunkered down for the night, sealed in against the storm.

Hey! *Hey!* someone shouted in my dream. The yelling got louder, then something wet grabbed my face. My hands went up. Uh-oh, I groaned, what the hell!? Searching around for my glasses, I peered up from the sleeping bag. Squinting, I thought I spotted nightday coming into the tent. What? a hole? Pulling off my covers I stood up on the wooden floor and right above my cot was a gaping opening framed by a ragged, dancing, orange-yellow flame.

"HEY—HEY GUYS—UP THERE—THE TENT IS BURNING."

Heads popped up from under pillows and covers.

"GODDAMN," someone said, "IT'S BURNING!!"

Shards of fine snow were pouring in through the widening gap. The sound was something like gurgled preaching.

Against all protocol, the last guy to tank had failed to shut off the two potbellied stoves. The wind had snapped one of the long metal heating tubes leading up through the roof. Aimed like a cannon, it was now shooting flames into the slanted canvas.

"SHUT OFF THE FUCKIN' STOVES, DAMMIT."

It was freezing. Nude and in shorts, we jumped around madly searching for anything liquid to dose the spreading fire. Remnants of water, juice, hot chocolate, Kool-Aid, and cans of beer rose into the air, falling back on our heads and swamping the tent. Shouts of "more . . . we need more" sent frantic searches for the only remaining fluid: scattered cans of beer. Being the tallest, Steve jumped up on a chair. With a can of beer in each hand like a western gun-fighter he squirted foamy beer up at the flames. "Fuck it, Steve, over there, over there, you're missing it!" Suds rained down on everything.

Then a fire alarm blasted through TRARG's compound.

Early the next morning, the C.O. entered to survey the damage. He silently scrutinized the jumbled mess. Huge splotches of juice, chocolate, lime, beer, and extinguisher fire chemicals created a Salvador Dali surrealistic picture. Plus a nauseous mixture hung on the canvas and saturated the wooden fixtures. None of us smelled much different.

The C.O. uttered not a word as he peered around the awful mess. Sniffing the air, though, he made a screwball face as he walked out, "Okay, let's get this cleaned up. Pronto! And the next time, whatever you men are mixing your booze with, don't even think of inviting me!"

PART THREE

August 1953

Outak

14

Dave's Letters to Wife Mike

Danes

❄ ✪ ❄

25 August 1953

Hello Darling,

I am dead tired, but what an eventful day. It all started as an ordinary morning. I prepared the Ice Cap Status Report for Joe and did some other duties. The day ended up with wonders seen and a very sunburned face. After I had gotten some work done, Dr. Benningoff, the botanist, arrived to obtain a clearance to go to Thule Village. At once the idea struck home. Capt. Page was not around, and this was my chance to go to the Danish and Eskimo Villages. I prepared the usual papers that were necessary to take to Commander Peterson, the Danish Liaison Officer. After I had gotten the batch ready, I took it over to have him sign it. He was not in and had gone to Labrador for business reasons. Hans, his assistant, said he was sure the scientist and his party would be able to go to the village. I asked if it were possible that I could go along. He said yes and I returned to Headquarters.

We set off for the Duck Dock and went over in Ducks (waterland vehicles) and arrived at the village twenty minutes later.

As we approached the village we could see the peaked houses come into view. They were painted in many different colors: red, purple, dark green, and yellow. The houses were so quaint and the architecture so unusual and rare. They remind one of the buildings in Norway and Sweden. Each house had a small solarium of glass

attached to the back. These were to grow plants or probably toma-
toes and other vegetables. Altogether there were about fifty houses
of many sizes. There is a large community building used for dancing
and evening get-togethers; a nice sized hospital, which is set apart
from the other buildings; a beautiful church in a maroon color; several
grain bins; and many little private houses. Eskimo dogs were tied up
in front or back of each house. All told it made a very nice village.

Overhead tower the cliffs of Mt. Dundas and North Mountain,
closing the village in a small valley of privacy and peace. Blond-haired
children running here and there in great excitement as our Duck neared
land. Each has fun watching the funny Americans. Eskimo children
mixed with the Danish children playing games as we came into view.
And then there were the Greenlander children (a cross between Danish and Eskimo). All seemed to be gay and in high spirits.

After looking around for several minutes, we loaded our gear of
backboards, cameras, and lunches to do botanical work at the empty
Eskimo village on the other side of the peninsula. As we passed the
outer group of houses, I noticed the decorative work and also the lack
of any city planning. Each house was apparently placed where the
owners wished it to be. It might be right next to a neighbor, or off in
the fields of rocks and flowers.

In the harbor there were small fishing and seal boats, and farther
out was a huge and beautiful Danish schooner. I have never seen any
like it before. Also a transport was unloading goods and food that the
villagers would need during the winter months. So the village was
surrounded with activities.

As we passed other houses, women were hanging out their wash,
and they were dressed in Greenland costumes as we had seen in a
movie about their king and queen. It was apparently a holiday with
the ships in the harbor.

It is very interesting to note that the Danish women had very
blond hair which was cropped in a boy style similar to Ingrid Berg-
man's in Joan of Arc. The Greenlanders had long dark brown or black
hair with braids down the back. The Eskimo women had long hair but
unbraided and hanging down the back.

We tramped out of the village and went past their little church, a reddish maroon color. A very unusual shape but quaint in appearance. Finally we cut across the slopes of Mt. Dundas and there we came across the old and empty Eskimo village.

This was an experience I shall never forget.

Your Loving Dave

Inuits

✳ ✪ ✳

3 September 1953

My Darling,

This time it's about the Inuits.

The huts are built of sod or rocks. In most cases the sod was piled up like we pile bricks. They are built along the sea and each has an entrance like that of an igloo. Since the village is located near this great and throbbing Air Base, the Eskimos managed to carry from the dump many things that could be used in building their homes. They had used boards and in many houses had lined the boarded walls with colored pictures from magazines. The houses only had one room and very small. One wonders where the family slept, ate, and did other evening chores—such as sex. I guess it all took place within the small space while all looked in.

The area was completely littered with junk and trash. Dr. Benningoff said these people are part of the Neolithic tribes of the world. Each hut we visited, and we went into many of them, was just as it had been when they left, which was apparently two months ago. They were littered with hair from the dogs and seal, bones, and grease from animals eaten raw, and many other unappetizing things. In fact one could say that the floors had about two to three inches of everything, from guts out of animals to the latest civilized mechanical thing, its purpose unknown to anyone but the Eskimos. Each house or hut smelled of rotted and sour seal skins from the animals killed and eaten.

Outside and next to the earth houses was a platform, about six or eight feet off the ground. This was so the dogs could not get to parts of the seals. The platforms are the storing unit for the household. The meat is kept there until ready to be eaten. There were several kayaks hanging from seal gut on small stands in front of the huts. They were interesting and we made a thorough investigation of them. We found many spears and harpoons, but all were too big to bring back to Thule AFB.

On our trip with us were two Danish scientists, both anthropologists. We were therefore able to get good detailed accounts of the habits of the tribes. We were told that this area is the best known for archeology of the study of Eskimos and that the history in the village goes back 1400 years. The Eskimo that Admiral [Robert E.] Peary used as a guide to the North Pole lived in this village, and of course, we were in his hut!

By this time it was noon and we were all hungry. We sat down along the shore and watched the icebergs floating around the harbor, and brought out our food. It was not much. We had ham and crackers, plus peanuts and fudge. Then while we were eating, we were startled

12. Dave at Outak's sod house.

to see a kayak swiftly moving in the water and heading toward us. A wizened old man got out and approached us. He was wearing seal-skins and colorful bandanas, and after greeting us, sat down. We offered him some of our food, and one of the anthropologists translated our conversation. It was a remarkable encounter.

But that will have to wait for another letter because it's getting very late and I'm bushed.

> Darling I miss you.
> Your Dave

The Encounter (Never Written to Mike)

"Let me get this straight." Once again I was soaked in envy. "You met who, exactly?"

He was still revved up from the day before. Lying sideways on his bunk, his arm pointing in the direction of the villages, Dave's impressions of his trip cascaded out. But when he mentioned Outak, the Inuit who had traveled with the French explorer Malaurie, I let out a whoop. Only several weeks earlier I had just finished reading *The Last Kings of Thule* and had recounted the alarm with which both men viewed the arrival of Thule Air Force Base. I couldn't believe he had actually met Outak. Dammit it, I thought, why wasn't I along on that trip?

"Joe, I'm trying to tell you. Don't rush me."

"Fuck it, Dave, I can't believe you met him. Outak. Are you sure?"

"That's what he called himself. One of the civilian scientists spelled out his name."

"What did he look like? Where was he coming from? What did he do while you were there? I mean, the village's abandoned, isn't it?"

"Joe," Steve admonished, "will you shut the fuck up and let Pogo continue his yakking!" Tom and Cupps sat at the edge of their bunks.

Dave seemed pleased. He was always telling me to slow down the words, occasionally offering a droll cut about Brooklyn. Which was amusing since I thought he spoke too slowly. In fact, I thought all my tent mates were in arrested conversational development, definitely backward in their talking pace. So much more could be said if only they spewed it out more quickly. They really didn't know any better and only turned off when I insinuated they should move it along. So I avoided saying, "spit it out," the prodding phrase of my Brighton Beach neighborhood.

"Hell, I don't know where he was coming from," continued Dave. "But, wow, there was something mysterious about the way he suddenly appeared, paddling in from the fjord. Which fits into my thinking that there is much mystery about this region of the world." Always the artist!

Dave's perception was right on target, and no one disputed it. Even disregarding the B-52s coming and going with their thermonuclear bombs, the terrain was seared immutably into our fantasies. It was as if it had always been this way down through all time.

No one interrupted after that.

"What does he look like? Well, he's very short, dark-skinned, his face creased rubbery and his black hair has wide, grayish streaks. He was wearing your typical Eskimo outfit made out of seal skin but," Dave smiled, "he had a very bright green bandana around his neck. A green bandana! So his face came through like a portrait. And he was beaming, as if he had a full sense of everything."

"Unbelievable," I sounded like an adolescent, "then what?"

"Okay, this is what happened. But, Joe, no more questions 'cause I'm trying to remember as much as possible, and it's kind of difficult. Outak spoke in both French and Eskimo, it was the scientist who did the interpreting. Who knows what was lost in the translation!

"After saluting us, in an affable way, he sat down on a boulder. We offered to share our food. He took some cheese and soda and thanked us. Pointing to the kayak, the scientist asked him if he had been fishing. He shook his head. Then he looked at us very closely and began talking in a very deliberate manner. This is the gist of what he said, or so the scientist translated roughly:

> I come with many messages from my people. We want you to know that
> we have left this place, our home, a difficult decision for us. I shall tell
> you why if you want to know.

I am back here now to look for some things, especially one that has disappeared, and seeing you on the beach I thought I would sit and talk with you. My name is Outak. May I know yours? Good.

For much time we watched the Americans build their base. In the beginning we were amazed. We could not have imagined such bigness, so many people and planes and ships. The constant noise, the scary sounds that went back and forth over the waters in the inlet. It disturbed us. It scared the walruses, the seals, the birds. It was not right.

And all this in such a small place!? We know there is hardly any land here. How could they do it? we asked. Where will they get the food they need, will they not starve? Will they hunt in our grounds and take the seals and fish and walruses and birds? We were very, very distressed. Many of us said that no good would come of all this.

Then we saw what was brought and we were happy. We watched the things grow high and then even higher. Are they throwing all this out? we asked. Not to be used any more? We did nothing for a while but when we saw that they didn't want it any longer we decided to explore.

So now clothing, boards, string, parts of knives, and other things are for us. Some things we did not need but we were pleased with them, like the broken mirrors and tools.

Many in the village said we were lucky to have those Americans here. Will they stay long? Then, over time, it began to get out of hand. It was too much, too much interruption in our lives, too much hunting around in the garbage, too much of you people coming into our village. Please don't be offended by my words, I like people, especially the French, but you want too much and you make so much noise.

Problems came. The walruses and seals and birds went away. Not all but so many that we had to paddle much further to get them. After last winter we held a big meeting. I was in favor of going to another place where we could be closer to hunting and wouldn't hear the planes any more. A very difficult thing to ask for.

The older people were in much favor, the younger ones were not so sure. For many days we talked and talked, then stopped, then talked some more. Finally we came to an understanding among us. It was time to go. We scouted for another place, another home.

Three weeks ago we collected our things, and moved. I am back now only for something that seems to be gone. I think I know what it is but I must be sure. I shall never come back again.

Do you understand? I trust so. It was good talking with you. Thank you for the food.

"With that," Dave inhaled wearily, "he got up and walked over to a hut. It was time for us to start back so we collected our stuff and got into the Duck. As we pulled away from the shore I looked but didn't spot him. His kayak was still there—apparently he was still in the hut." He paused momentarily and clasped his hands over his head.

"Just maybe, though, he wasn't back for some item like he said but wanted one last reflection, a kind of meditation with his past. I think so because of the way he spoke. I think he wanted to tell himself something special. And I think also that he wanted us to know something special."

Nobody spoke for what seemed like a long stretch. Then Steve stood up and put on his parka. "What I need most in this world," he uttered to himself, "is to get the fuck out, out of this fucking tent."

I laid down on my bunk and thought, why shouldn't this go into the history? And I immediately knew the answer: it won't because it doesn't matter to anyone but the Inuits, Dave, and me plus a few others who care, but I also thought less cynically, maybe, maybe.

15

Ice Cap Nemesis

Ron and the Crevasses

Assessing, plotting, and mounting an armada to the Top of the World and then down the other side was, to put it mildly, akin to madness. Before any large-scale operation could be put into position, exploration of every type had to cleave its way past innumerable obstacles. This was, after all, the secret raison d'être of TRARG's existence. Yet even constructing the tiny jumping-off Nuna Takeoff Camp at the edge of the ice cap proved to be a major feat in itself.

Crucial swings from the main camp began the minute the weather eased. Early convoys of sledded tracked machines chugged up the icy fjord, up tundra ramps, and then up onto the ice cap, with uncertainties looming at every snow-inch of the way.

The ice cap rises in a flattened dome shape to a maximum altitude of ten thousand feet, an immense mass of approximately 830,000 square miles. Glaciers pushing downward flow to the ocean or end abruptly in ice cliffs hundreds of feet high. At its outer fringes, the seasonal thawing of snow and ice over uneven bedrock creates melting streams pouring into underground rivulets. These in turn produce subterranean crevasses of all sorts of sizes and depths. And as everyone knew, locating the pesky crevasses was crucial to the entire mission.

In its initial foray one year earlier, TRARG had been directed to move supplies from Thule to a US–Denmark weather station on the ice cap, hundreds of miles out, then under construction. Starting its trek in April, barely the end of winter, a heavy sled convoy came to a precipitous halt when tractors and equipment broke through submerged snow-bridged crevasses. They were scarcely fourteen miles from Thule.

Reconnaissance helicopters can easily spot the exposed crevasses but the tricky, concealed ones require technical monitoring that was not then developed. TRARG experimented with an instrument based on certain principles of seismology and initially the procedure was partially effectual. Yet it didn't locate them all; far too many were elusive. On more than one occasion the calm surface was deceptive, and a snow tractor dove right in. Most of the vehicles were extricated but some just disappeared into the maw.

Cautiousness dictated, and so it became necessary to take mechanical readings every few feet. That really slowed things down, so much so that to accomplish the mighty task of getting over to Greenland's other shore was virtually impossible.

13. Octopus crevasse locator. Courtesy of US Army Transportation Museum.

Problem: how to speed up the operation? Ingenuity was ruled out and human expendability was ruled in. Solution: an individual on skis tethered to the lead weasel via a long nylon rope poked along every few feet with a long pole. When the pole went deep there was a reasonable chance that a crevasse existed, if it didn't, well, there was more certainty that it was clear of crevasses. On the other hand, one man with one pole doesn't carry much weight, so the man on skis wasn't exactly an accurate barometer either.

Draftee Ron, the tallest man in the outfit and an electronic engineer to boot, was selected for this choice assignment. He guided many a convoy up the ice cap. Bets were taken in the Three Ps about his longevity. He made sure his G.I. insurance was paid up.

Troublesome for the convoys as well were ground surface conditions. Winter temperatures dropping as low as –90 Fahrenheit mixed

14. Mapping the ice cap. Courtesy of US Army Transportation Museum.

with endless blizzards creating small waves like ocean water coming ashore on a beach. Travel in weasels and wanigans—a house on a sled for crew quarters—were not for those with delicate stomachs or weak kidneys. Machine breakdowns were not uncommon, and the ice cap was not exactly a place where you want to get marooned even for short periods of time. Eventually, of course, convoys made it through the crevasse fields.

Topographer Gallant's Swing, 12 August

To: Office of the Historian, Cpl Boskin
Date: August 12, 1953
From: Raymond Gallant, Cartographer and Topographer, Civilian
Status Report: "Preliminary Report on Ice Cap Travel: Cartography and Geodesy"

Dear Joe:

My part in the expedition was, in addition to assisting the party chief and acting as ice cap technician, to do cartography, topography and geodesy. In discharging these duties, I assumed the responsibility of leading the weasel train in zones known to be dangerous. Preparing for the zones, we brought along nylon climbing rope, ice axes, crampons, probes, pitons, parachute harnesses, and cables to pull weasels.

Reconnaissance by air before our swing departure revealed excellent conditions. The route followed was the same as last year. Thick snow bridges covered the few crevasses we crossed, and no difficulties were encountered. The weasel train moved in single file when in zones of hard snow and in two columns when the snow was soft. As we moved to a higher elevation, no crevasses were met but we encountered an irregular zone due to ablation (net loss of snow or ice by melting or wind action or evaporation during a specific period of time) which is about 1/2 miles wide and parallel to the margin.

Our party stayed at the destination from July 20 to August 12, during which time I worked on astronomical fixes, glaciological profiles, and snow measurement. In general, bad visibility hampered operations but the temperature varied from 25 F to 47 F.

Despite the weather difficulties, I made profiles of the margin of the ice cap and also a map of a segment of the land on a scale of 1:20,000. In addition to astronomical fixes and triangulation, important points can be used to make a map from aerial photographs.

We plan to begin our journey back to Nuna Takeoff Camp tomorrow, and if the weather holds up should be back within the week. Look forward to talking to you at that time.

Respectfully,
Ray

Gallant's Swing, One Week Later

"Ron, what the fuck happened?—some of it we already know!"

News had spread quickly and everyone was talking about it. We waited in the Three Ps for Ron to make it back from Nuna Takeoff Camp. What filtered down was that a disaster had occurred to Ray Gallant's weasel expedition on its return to base. The caravan passed over a sizeable, previously mapped crevasse that was assumed solid. But after the lead weasel had passed over it, the second one plunged in, perching precariously at its lip at a forty-degree angle. Secured in their safety belts, the two men inside were initially unhurt but their situation was ominous. Getting them out swiftly without further nudging the weasel would be touch-and-go.

A strong wind was again blowing shards of rock against the sides of the tent; otherwise there was a hush inside. Nobody spoke as Ron gave us a detailed run-down:

"From the lead vehicle, standing about twenty yards from the crevasse, we lowered two nylon ropes down to the weasel. The guys carefully opened up the doors and tied the ropes to their waists. We figured to haul them up one at a time. The closest guy to the crevasse wall going first since the weasel was leaning in that direction. We got him out pretty easily and thought this might ease up on the weasel's incline—but no sooner was he out than the weight-loss tipped it downward. And then the son-of-a-bitch snow-lip began to give way.

"With the other guy still attached, we moved the lead weasel backward to allow some room to maneuver—but couldn't get too close because of the unknown size of the crevasse. Meanwhile, the guy was being buffeted against the side of the vehicle. When he tried to get out, it pitched further downward.

"Everyone was shouting, hollering to move the lead weasel closer so's to give him some more slack, shouting for him to get the fuck out before it completely goes, just get the fuck out, get out.

"The guy was straining to push through the door but he was also being shoved down at the same time. Then at the last second as the weasel went kablooey, the guy swung free and we hauled him up. But, but—in any case we never heard the crash, that's how deep it was. Just an eerie silence."

No one could speak.

15. Blizzard conditions. Courtesy of US Army Transportation Museum.

Dave had more questions. "What are all the 'buts' about? We already know the guy was hurt but don't know how much. It's sort of been hushed up. Who is he anyway?"

"Well," said Ron looking abjectly, "the poor guy lost the lower half of his right arm getting out, a lot of blood, and also a hell of a lot of skin on his face and head. He almost bled to death but we managed to get a tourniquet on him and stopped it. Luckily for him the weather held up and the 'copter got there real fast, otherwise—who knows?

"It's Jim, Jim McCracken, a regular who's been in for about fifteen years. Most of you don't really know him. He's been at the Nuna Takeoff Camp for almost the entire time. I've been on several swings with him. A really good man who truly knows his stuff."

We all just sat there, slowly shaking our heads, partly in commiseration for McCracken who we barely knew. This was a small outfit and a

16. Rescuing a vehicle from a crevasse. Courtesy of US Army Transportation Museum.

tight camaraderie had grown over the many months. Though no one said it directly, everyone felt fortunate that it wasn't him in that weasel.

"Hey, Ron," Tom asked, "are you back here for good or are you scheduled for another swing?"

Ron grimaced. "I've had it, period. Let 'em send Steve."

Guffaws and eyes turned to Steve. To our surprise he passed over a Shakespearean opportunity. Instead he burst into a popular song, "I'm Walking Behind You."

PART FOUR

September–November 1953

Over and Out

SCENE 4

PLACE: C.O.'s Atwell
TIME: Mid-September, late evening
WEATHER: Early winter: sun dipping down, moon up, winds accelerating

CHARACTERS

C.O. BALSTRUM
CPL. BOSKIN

Subject: History of the Operation

C.O.: Boskin, just how far along are you?
CPL.: Well, sir, I would say almost everything is in order to begin the writing soon after we're back at Fort Eustis.
C.O.: I'm not referring to the files, Boskin . . . I know you've been working and organizing them over the past five months. I'm referring to our conversations about the history of the mission. Have you given more thought to our recent discussions?
CPL.: Sir, we just don't see eye-to-eye about this matter. History is not something you trifle with. As I've said, it's crucial to get it all down as accurately as possible. Facts are like jewels, they're precious—
C.O.: Boskin, you still don't get it! Knock off the jewels metaphor . . . unless you're referring to mine, which you'd better not be! Don't you realize who's going to be reading this history of OURS?

CPL.: Well, yes, sir, I know damned well, which is why . . .

C.O.: Boskin, since you know damned good and well who the people are, stop snowing me. Remember you're not going to be the only person interpreting or judging things here—you're just the goddamn historian! And you're just one person!

CPL.: Sir, what I know is that when this history comes out, trained persons will be siphoning through the facts and collating them—and they're going to know whether the wool is being shoved over their eyes. If you leave things out, or skew them, then everything we learned up here is lost. And future expeditions can't learn from our mistakes . . .

C.O.: What mistakes?! Are you coming back here next year? Isn't your glorious stint over before then, Corporal? Or, maybe, just maybe I could send through a request for an extension of duty!

CPL.: Wow, not necessary, sir. But I have to point out I have a real stake in this. My integrity is on the line, for one. Another is that I want a history that says something real important. The future makes no sense unless the past is accounted for.

C.O.: Oh, spare me all the rhetoric you learned in college courses! Hell, accountability . . . so do I want it, so does the Company want it, so does the Pentagon want it, so do future expeditions want it. So let's make sure we're going down history's road together on this! I can assure you, you'll be traveling with me in the front seat—but not behind the wheel. Beside me, Corporal, ah yes, beside me . . . You can whisper in my ear all you want. But take it from me, Boskin, no more than that—just a goddamn whisper!!

16

Curving Down, Hauling Out

"Can You Believe No Bitching . . . ?!"

The furious, far-reaching, incongruous summer was almost over. It was early September. The season had lasted much longer than anyone anticipated. In the previous year, so the weather guys smugly informed us, there were at least two feet of snow on the ground by that time.

The climate-switch in the great sky suddenly clicked. The upper atmosphere went pallid, the air sliced sharper, the wind widened its message, and the moon and sun competed with each other for hanging time. No one bet on the sun.

Time became the company's true enemy. Not that it was ever that friendly. At the most, just a month remained before the winter would move in to reclaim what it had temporarily lost.

Orders went out for every available body, including mine, including Steve's, to move over to the base Nuna Takeoff Camp. I balked at yet another helicopter horror. This time, however, the larger H-19 craft carried our group over.

Regardless, I had my eyes closed the entire trip.

Takeoff Camp was akimbo with equipment strewn all around and the roads rutted in permafrost quagmire. Morale was an unspeakably dirty word. Months earlier the bitching had been upbeat, a bantering tone. At that time the mission was bustling, the experiments pushed imaginations, and the purpose remained elevated. Not any longer.

Frustrations were palpable. Everyone was in a surly, dyspeptic mood. Eyes avoided, and when they met, there was a smoldering intensity. Conditions were so bad, exclaimed Dave perceptively, that "no one even

153

bitched about anything." About the only expression screeching above the wind was FUCK/FUCK!! and if really pissed, GET OFF MY FUCKING BACK!!

Frenzied work went on around the clock. Some cracked under the strain and were instantly dubbed "the lucky bastards" when the helicopter transferred them to the base hospital. Then it began to snow, and snowed Greenland-style, a divine show. Tiny, translucent névé flakes drifted down ever so nimbly, caressing the quagmire and our thoughts as well. Running into Steve on the way to the privy, I was bestowed a Shakespearean quote cued to the changing scene: "'The white cold virgin snow upon my heart / Abates the ardour of my liver,' *The Tempest*, Act IV, Scene 1." He had come prepared.

Instead of speeding up, though, everyone slowed down. We would be getting out of there soon enough.

"Dear Mrs. Landers . . ."

"Dear Mrs. Landers," Dave wrote to Mike a.k.a. the advice columnist, "I have a problem: how does one get out of this chicken-shit Army?"

It was Dave's birthday, and he was morose. He wanted to share his feelings with me though we hadn't been getting along too well. Over the long summer we had had ups and downs. He got on my nerves, I on his. We weren't an odd couple because we had much in common. Rather it was the intensity, the pace that rarely allowed breathing space. There were only a few ways to dissemble, and no place to hide. We were figuratively stark naked, and this being the Arctic meant really being out in the psychological cold.

Getting mail to Takeoff Camp had always been tricky but the ongoing terrible storm stopped all incoming helicopter flights. Dave was unabashedly pining for Mike. I felt the time had finally come to pull out my secret stash. On the eve of departing for Thule, a coquettish woman I had been dating gave me a bottle of cherry cordial, the first word, she playfully explained, symbolic of our coming together. She didn't want me to forget, she exclaimed with a final gleeful twist. As it turned out, I didn't.

Three of us were crowded into a tiny Atwell. The other was Crevasse Ron who was in the know about the run of ice cap experiments. There was no way, he said ruefully, "no fucking way, to locate the myriad of criss-crossing crevasses." Not radar or sonar nor nothing electronic had consistently worked, given the pesky types of crevasses. So they resorted to guys like poor Ron attached by nylon rope to a lead weasel poking along in the deep snow. Ron had had his share of plunging into enough crevasses to last several lifetimes. And there was no category for being scared out of one's wits, no psychological Purple Heart here.

This intractable problem had enormous ramifications. What it meant was that it would be unfeasible to mount an extensive caravan of tracked vehicles filled with multitudes of men and equipment over the ice cap. Consequently, I surmised, there would be no air force base on the other side of Greenland. Thule was as close as the Strategic Air Command (SAC) would get atop the world to vanquish the Enemy's heart. Until the deployment of missiles, Moscow would remain about five flying hours away.

At least this was my interpretation of TRARG's top-secret stratagem but neither Ron nor Dave wholly subscribed to it. "Where did you read in any of the reports," Dave had challenged more than once, "that our ultimate objective is to determine whether it's feasible to head over the ice cap to construct another base closer to the Soviet Union!?"

This time I couched my case with debater's care. "I know there's absolutely nothing in the original documents that indicates the Pentagon's main aim. As usual, it's hidden in the jargon, and in our case it's overblown with scientific gobbledygook. No offense. But, look, nothing else makes sense. What are they really trying to figure out here?? Why all this scientific exploration from so many military quarters and angles, so many scientists from other countries, so many site visits from the bigwigs in Washington? Why all the high-class expertise draftees along with the regular specialists? Our outfit may be small but our objectives are huge. Other than the DEW line, there's no reason to mount supply trains onto the ice cap over such great distances. Hell, the DEW boys can be continually supplied, as they are now, by airdrops."

Dave and Ron were good listeners, I have to say that for them. Either that, or like the rest of us, they were plain worn down and caught up in the minutia of workday obstacles. After months of turmoil, perhaps they too had entered into the swelling ranks of hardened cynics. Or maybe it was that I had spoken so rapidly and passionately, they just couldn't get a word in edgewise.

Plus, they were not exactly convinced. "For Pete's sake," Ron said in an exasperated tone, "we're draftees, peons, just about the lowest rank in the military. Even though this is a top-secret outfit and you're the historian and Dave is intelligence, we don't know . . . Only the brass really knows what's up, and they're not exactly forthcoming. And I bet, yeah, I bet, what's up doesn't amount to a hill of beans," he paused trying to be cute, "or a mound of snow."

I didn't laugh. I was in my historian's mode. "So your take on all of this," I asked heatedly, "is what? What exactly does mound of snow mean??"

"Joe, all they want to know is how to fight a war on snow and ice. Meaning, up here or in Alaska or both. Now that I think of it, the Antarctic, also—though yeah that's probably stretching my point too far. But I don't think getting onto the ice cap and going to the other coast has anything to do with building another air base, it's more like they see the next war as geologically total. The fighting, they figure, will take place in any and every type of terrain."

"Is this your take, Dave? Do you agree with Ron?" I asked plaintively. Dave sort of nodded and shrugged at the same time.

Undeterred, I reached down deeper to bolster my thesis.

"Plenty of arctic explorers over the decades have noted the insurmountable problem of moving around on the ice cap. So why does the Pentagon now think otherwise? Because their arrogance tells them that new technologies can solve these huge difficulties? Could be that, yeah, sure. Sometimes it works but more often it fails because the technology is puny against nature.

"No, what I think is that having bases all over the world squeezed against the Soviet Union fits right into the policy of containment laid down by George Kennan. And it also has everything to do with preventing another Pearl Harbor. SAC's going to make sure the Soviets get the point by being so surrounded by Air Force bases that they'd never consider striking us. Retaliation would be instantaneous from all over the world. So they're inching to get closer to the Soviet Union, on the other side of Greenland, only a couple of hours away from Moscow. They literally want to be breathing down their necks! So fuck the cost."

Somehow they didn't quite buy it. "Well," said Ron thoughtfully, "it sounds somewhat plausible but I still have my doubts. But what I do know is that they won't admit failure because that would end all funding. We've certainly learned a hell of a lot about the arctic militarily, so they should be able to finesse more."

It was time for Dave's birthday.

Cherry Cordial Caterwauling

"Ron," I whispered, leaning over, "it's Dave's birthday, and I have a secret stash." Even if Ron wasn't finished talking, I was impatient. Dave was too downcast.

"A secret what?"

"I've been carrying a bottle of cherry cordial since we left the States," I said rather proudly, ". . . been waiting for the right moment to trot it out. Now seems like just the right moment."

"My god," Dave looked up, "how'd you manage without breaking it— or even drinking it?"

"Well I have to admit I took a few nips now and then, but hey, nothing major. And I felt kind of guilty even drinking that!" Below the bunk I reached for my duffel bag and deep inside found the small rounded bottle with its long snout. Both Ron and Dave let out a snickered laugh. I looked at it tenderly, pulled out the cork, and cheerily belted out happy birthday to Dave. Ron chimed in.

I handed it over to Dave. "Joe," he swigged, "it's heavenly." He passed it over to Ron, who being bigger, took a bigger gulp.

No one said a word, just quaffed it down and down.

Uh-oh, I thought, this bottle is on the way out.

A sudden burst of wind made us jump. The bottle disappeared behind someone's back. Who the hell was coming? "We're getting paranoid," said Ron. "Fuckin' A," I retorted. The bottle went around again.

Now we three were not exactly frontline drinkers. And being at the Nuna Takeoff Camp had separated us from our intimate buddies. We

hadn't had a beer in many days, and the real drinkers, mostly the regulars, were hoarding their own stuff. So even though the cordial didn't
have much alcoholic kick, it went to work real fast. Within minutes we
were fairly schnockered.

Laughing like school kids we passed the bottle around and around
hopefully enticing yet another drop out. "God, do I detest this place," said
Ron, his long arms flaying. "I've had all the bullshit I can take. It's time to
get out of here. Any more in the bottle?"

"Nope, s'all gone, and I think so's Dave."

I whacked Dave's knee. His feet were on the floor but the rest of him
was sprawled backward on the bunk, an arm over his eyes. He wasn't
totally out, because suddenly I heard him gently weeping. "Dave," I mur-
mured, "I'm sorry if I was a bastard this week. It's just that I'm fed up.
Please, it's your birthday."

Everything looked a bit blurry in the cramped Atwell. Unexpectedly,
Dave jumped up like a whooping crane about to take flight. His voice was
a bit choked. "For Chrissake, it has nothing, nothing to do with any of
you. I miss my Mike, MY MIKE. It's my birthday and you and Ron are poor
substitutes. I'm sorry." He really was into his cups. Then he whooped, "I
wanna go HOME, please take me back HOME." He sat down on the floor.

Ron and I looked at each other. "I think," said Ron, "maybe we should
get the hell out of here."

"Yeah," I shouted willingly.

"No," explained Ron, "I mean let's raid the mess and see if there's any
cake around. Let's tell everyone it's Dave's birthday. Hell, fuck the snow,
let's GO!"

Choir Boys

We grabbed our parkas and gloves and busted out into the bending snowy
wind. "Let us in, by the hair of our chinny-chin-chin," sing-song shouted
Ron, pounding on a small door across the small tundra street. No one
heard us. He grabbed the storm-proof handle and pushed the door open.
No one was in there. "What the fuck, empty!"

"Onto the next!"

Down the road was a larger Atwell. The mindless wind blew us right against the door. "Open up," Ron yelled and knocked with both fists, "or by the hair of my chinny-chin-chin, we'll blow the place in." Laughing, we hammered together.

The door abruptly swung open. A grinning face peered at us and waved us in. Upwards of five guys were in there, all in a gleeful state. Not a one of them was sober.

"Hey, lookie-lookie who's here. It's Crevasse Ron and his two choir boys, the historian and his buddy the intelligence man." It was our Thule tent-mate Sexton with a den of regulars. "Hey, sit down ol' buddies—but not for too long."

"Sexton, fuck off," I replied, making doubly sure it sounded play-ful. "You guys have the privilege of our company because it's a special occasion. Not everyone in the outfit has this opportunity and we chose you-all"—my futile attempt at a Texas accent that always brought smirks—"because of your good looks."

"Yeah," added Ron quickly, "and also because of your stash."

"Oh, yeah, tell us choir-boy historian, just what's this special occasion!"

"Okay, I'll tell, provided you-all keep it a secret."

"Right," piped Dave jocularly, "a very top-secret."

"For your information, and for your ears only," I hesitated, then shouted, "Hey-Hey, it's Dave's birthDAY! Can you believe it, he just turned eighteen—he just looks twenty-two because of this wonderful climate."

"No shit," said a voice, "your birthday, Dave?! Hell, ah luv birthdays. Fuck-it-all, who-all doesn't love birthdays?! Whoever-all doesn't love birth-days is an asshole." These guys were long-gone sheets to the arctic wind.

Several bottles were right on a small round table! Coffee mugs were thrust into our hands. Clinks resounded. Everyone raised their cups and shouted a happy birthday to Dave. For the first time in days he was smil-ing. He swiftly gulped down his drink. I did the same and tears rolled up in my eyes, not from Dave's changed mood but from the ninety-proof bourbon.

"You guys are the best choir boys," were the last words I heard from Sexton as I staggered back with Dave to our quarters.

Crevasse Ron stayed behind. He was just getting warmed up.

17

Directly into Dusk

A Horrifying Thought

One day the sun returned for a light-hearted visit; on the next day it was chased away by its nemesis, darkness. Soon the sun would be heading elsewhere in its global itinerary, and darkness would bed down for a long while.

It was time for the company to pack it in, no mean task.

Doubts mingled with disarray. Conceived as a two-year project, TRARG was supposed to return the following year for additional ice cap experiments. Large equipment was placed into hibernation in a cavernous supply depot, a skeleton crew left behind to oversee details over the winter months. How they were supposed to maintain psychological equilibrium was never posed. They were all regulars.

Everything else went back, top-secret files, hundreds of maps, minor scraps of paper, and at the last moment, the geologist's Battleship game. Every item, I argued, was needed for the final report to the Pentagon for their deliberations.

Once again, we boarded the monstrous cargo airplane and the engine's roar instantly and completely stunned our hearing. As the plane rose into a crystalline sky, the whitish landscape seared our eyes. Dave and I glanced at each other, hit each other on the shoulder, and shrugged a spontaneous, silent FUCK IT, followed by a silent laugh.

On everyone's mind was a horrifying thought: would we be back in six months?!

Beholder's Art/Beholder's History

"What's up? How come you're looking so gloomy? We're getting out of here today."

We had just turned in our gear to Supply Rich and were lying on the bare, hard springs of tent cots. Next stop, the airport runway. Dave was whistling. I was churning.

"I'm fucking anxious."

"What about? Women? Afraid your crossed letters have cost you a female or two?"

"Well, that's for sure. I've screwed up at least once in letters and presents. I tell you, Dave, I envy you, being married takes the edge out of frustration. I don't know who the hell I can con into bed when I get back. But no, that's not it. I'm anxious about the history."

"The history? You're worrying about that?!"

"Dave, what the hell am I going to write when I have to compile the final report? What the hell am I going to write??"

Dave understood but I didn't blame him for sloughing it off a bit. I knew he was as deeply pissed by the ineptitude and ill-conceived nature of the whole affair as I was. Yet Dave saw the world through the eyes of an artist. He drew it straight or round, upside down or inside out, any way his imagination took him. Exactitude had nothing to do with it. He could dip into any can of paint or watercolors, and let the brush fly, the emerging picture taking form as mind's eye grappled with space.

Or so I thought. Maybe this was shortsighted on my part. My artistic references were extremely limited, if not downright shallow. What propelled my concern had to do with making certain that the ensuing history would not be compromised by others, particularly the C.O. or any of the other officers. And certainly not by me! All the papers I had previously written, including my master's thesis, were bounded by scholarly values. Where the facts led, so the historian shall tread. Interpretation arose from the bedrock sources, footnotes pinpointing time and place. Isn't this what had been drilled in my seminars, the comments on my papers demanding previous insightful works by recognized first-rate minds? How would this be possible in this situation??

Yet, I also knew that while both art and history were separate, they were also inseparable, both prismatic visions seeking comprehension. Even the history I wanted to write had an artistic side to it—if you can call it that—namely my own serious questions about US policies toward the Soviet Union and the Cold War itself.

"What concerns you so much? That you won't be able to put down all the ins and outs, the errors and stupidities, that happened?"

"Right, plus what we talked about all the time. The cost of another military base—what a rip-off!—against the social needs of society. Making sure this doesn't happen again. You and I both know the C.O. is going to snow-white the report—hey, that's a pretty funny take on Walt Disney." My anxieties were clearly getting the better of me.

"So what do I do, write my own secret report about a secret outfit? Even if I could do it, I wouldn't know who to give it to. Who the hell would publish it?

"And if I ever did, lord knows what would happen to me. Oh fuck it, I'll just wing it. But it sickens me."

"Look," Dave said consolingly, "I suggest you hold onto all the files and one day write it up. I'll try to do the same."

A horn sounded. A batch of us jumped into the truck heading to the monstrous cargo plane to cart us back to Fort Useless, Virginia.

Dave Freaks Out

Dave and I split up. With the bulk of the outfit, I traveled directly to our home base in Virginia. With the congenial officer in charge of the Intelligence Division, Dave went straight to Washington, D.C. Well, more or less, as it turned out. The pair had orders to transport the company's vital top-secret files to a specified office in the Pentagon. What happened next is not to be believed but then again the not to be believed is what makes history leap into the wondrously incongruous. It was the closest Dave ever came to court-martial for violating regulations, and perhaps even aiding and abetting the Enemy. He later recounted the harrowing faux pas:

Captain Seb Hoberts and I flew from Thule Air Force Base to Westover Air Force Base, outside of Springfield, Massachusetts. There we took a train to New York City, and after much protest from myself, slightly diverged from our scheduled plans. We decided on a pit stop in the city. It had been too long in the frozen wastes not to avail ourselves of the grandeur of the City.

So we checked our TOP SECRET attaché cases in several luggage lockers in Grand Central Station. This was strictly a breach of security and I tried to convince the Captain of taking them with us but he was insistent on catching up with life. And he is such a mild-mannered guy!

We then took off to see the town. Little did I realize how much alcohol Hobbie would, and did drink. I must add that I also consumed much more than I usually do. We dined at a great restaurant, and after a long evening in several bars, headed back to Grand Central Station to retrieve the files.

But somewhere along the way we lost the keys. Who knows where!? And we didn't record the numbers. We were aghast and searched futilely for the lockers. We explained the problem to the station-master, pleading with him about opening up the lockers with a master key, but he refused to do it without special permission from the police. We didn't know what to do. Exhausted, we gave up and boarded the train for Washington, then onto Williamsburg and Fort Eustis.

We no sooner got into our private sleeping compartments than Hobbie, beside himself, stated that he was going to the club car for a nightcap. He just couldn't sleep knowing that his ass would be mounted in the Pentagon, or at the prison in Fort Leavenworth. I was also so shaken up that I couldn't accompany him for more drinks.

At least that's what I thought I did. However, the next morning we both awoke somewhere near Richmond with heads slightly more expanded than normal. I departed the train in Williamsburg and Hobbie continued to Fort Eustis. He looked like a ghost when we split up.

Today I am not clear about what happened to the TOP SECRET documents which we were carrying. It is possible that FBI agents met us in Washington, D.C. I somehow think they knew of the situation because no one ever said a word to either of us, so it's pretty certain that the Pentagon came into the possession of the files.

What I do know is that when I debarked in Williamsburg I bumped into a neighbor as I got off the train. Her first words to me were: "Does your wife know you are coming back? She certainly has had a number of young men visiting her while you were gone." She was not aware that my wife had written to me about each of the male friends of mine who visited with her, and often took her out to dinner. But can you imagine the snoopiness of neighbors?? This lady could have wrecked my marriage!

Oh So Wonderful Being Back with Women Again!

I reached for a pay telephone at each quick stop along the way back to Fort Eustis. I was not alone. The outfit was a swarm of bees hooked on the honey of the phone call.

As we traveled by a pre-air-conditioning train from New England to Virginia in late fall, the East Coast was sweltering in a heat wave and it became hotter still as we headed south. Still outfitted in arctic gear, our blood hovering at the boiling point, the itching almost total, uncontrollable; our thick, bushy moustaches tingled, jumping around our lips.

Sentries patrolled Fort Useless. It was late at night when we pulled in. Instead of heading directly back to TRARG quarters, however, we were transported to an unfamiliar sector at the very edge of the camp. "Where're they taking us?" a tired, angry voice asked in the troop truck. "Who the fuck knows!?" someone replied. "Wait," I said, "I think I know. During basic training they assigned me to guard duty at the WAC barracks. This looks like it!"

Sure enough. Adjacent to the WAC compound were several decrepit World War II buildings. We tumbled out of the trucks, by that time not giving a hoot about where we were, close to women or not. Staggering inside, we sagged down at the nearest cot and collapsed into deep sleep.

Twenty minutes later, or so it seemed, reveille sounded. Not a body budged. I don't think anyone had even made it to the john during the night. "Okay," came the intrusive voice from up somewhere, "let's move it. You guys are back home now. Welcome to civilization! Aren't you happy!" It was Sexton, our tent-mate regular buddy now reverting to his old regular army self.

Achingly, everyone roused up, bitching like hell. Reluctantly donning the thick, crawly, arctic clothing, we walked like mummies, some guys even managing a trek to the bathroom. Shoved outside, desultory lines formed, everyone looking down at the strange ground. Then suddenly we spotted leaves dangling from branches. "What odd-looking trees," said someone sardonically. The glaring sun cringed our eyes. It was jarringly Virginia humid. A bit wobbly himself, Sexton glanced upward and mur-mured what for him was a gentle request, "Men, I hate to do this to you but you gotta police the area."

Groans voiced up in unison. "Hey, Sex," shouted a guy, "don't exactly recall, what's this so-called policing?" Another chirped in, "Sexton, are you fuckin' kiddin'!? Police this fuckin' area?? It's a hellhole!"

"That's an order," said Sexton, a bit more forcibly but still playful.

It was a hellhole all right, the bare, hardened earth filled with pits, rocks, and butts, the barracks looking even worse in the daylight. The adjacent WAC buildings were the opposite, impeccably white and not a nick or smudge marring them. An odd juxtaposition that made no sense except that this was the military.

More than a few guys expressed dismay, pledging that they were going to file a complaint about the situation. "Women shouldn't have to live next door to this shit. They shouldn't be treated this way, no-way," someone shouted.

We fanned out, shuffling along as if chains hung on our legs. Not a soul reached down to pick up a butt or scrap. Rocks, though, were another matter: these were empathetically booted. Grunts and yawns punctured fractured conversations.

Suddenly came the sounds of windows hoisting up. Everyone halted and turned in the direction of the WAC quarters. Women!! For so long we had only dreamed of them. Now there were women in the windows! Women leaning out from both floors! Women looking directly at us! After those long, long months, a blessed sight! Angels in uniform! We straight-ened up, swiftly patted down our moustaches, smoothed down our hair.

Instinctively, our hands collectively shot up, and rustling like a field of wheat in the wind, waved back-and-forth to them.

A female voice sang out. "All right, you guys," she chirped merrily, "all we want to see is ASSHOLES and ELBOWS!!"

A cannon shot across the ship's bow, she had topped us cold. Mouths opened and chuckled anxiously. Only Steve was up to the moment. "Oh," he declared sardonically, "it's so good to be back with *women* again!"

"C'mon Steve," I offered, "you can do better than that."

"Right—right." Shielding his eyes from the sun, Steve bowed in the direction of the voice and loudly intoned:

> Take, O take those lips away,
> that so sweetly were foresworn;
> And those eyes, the break of day,
> Lights that do mislead the morn.
> *Measure for Measure* . . . all you gentlewomen!

PART FIVE

Epilogue

May 2001

Sometimes Time Is Inconsequential

It had been nearly forty years since we had last seen each other.

The roads are so confusing around Boston that I couldn't give easy directions, so I suggested that we meet at a hotel entrance. Eager, I jogged most of the way there.

A tangle of thoughts balled up. Delight and curiosity vied with uncertainty. Which was another reason I jogged. I couldn't stand thinking about what it would be like after so many light years apart. A weekend, but of what? What is to be expected, what left unspoken, between two friends initially thrown together by a wartime episode?

In the immediate years after Thule, there were gatherings at respective graduate schools, then lively correspondence and occasional talks over the phone, and then silence between us. Not unusual for Americans who often share an intimate encounter followed by removal.

But Dave was never far removed from my thoughts. On the contrary, his artistic demeanor stayed fixed within me, and several of his wall-entrancing tapestries bound me to his presence. Early on, with funds sparse, I purchased several of Dave's early works. They became the artifacts of my own personal history. When they yellowed, I put them into cylindrical container tubes and stashed them with other memorabilia.

Yet as was the case with others poking back into their past at the close of the twentieth century, the Internet reunited us. E-mail picked up where voices had been dormant. Still, it was obviously not the same as being in the same space.

My thoughts raced faster than my jogging. I knew they wouldn't look as I had remembered, yet I wanted them to. Would I be so foolish as not to recognize them? Hell, how will I strike them?? I pray they'll look grand, Dave artistically ethereal and Mike sensuously lovely. I didn't want to be disappointed. Hell, I didn't want to disappoint them! All these feelings were the nervous afflictions everyone possesses on their way to a reunion.

They were waiting in the car and watched my winded dash into the hotel's circular entrance. Dave popped out and threw out his arms. Having just recuperated from a triple-bypass operation, Mike waved through the glass. Unlike the icebergs, the years instantly melted. They were beautiful. I shouldn't have fretted. Sometimes time is inconsequential.

Thule Tapestry

Every remembrance save Thule was revived. It wasn't until dinner that I finally pushed back to the Three Ps. "It's rather intriguing, don't you think," I anxiously began, "that Thule forced its way into our thoughts at about the same time. Just when I was sorting out my tattered notes, you were compiling the letters you wrote to Mike. What do you think triggered it off?"

Dave was already into his third wine, so I reminded him of his condition at the Nuna Takeoff Camp. For a moment there was no connection, then he laughed. "Well, I can handle spirits much better now—much practice over the years. But to your question. Thule never left me, and apparently not you either. Something always gnawed at me but I could never quite put my finger on it. When Mike found my old letters to her—her letters to me somehow have disappeared—I thought here was a chance to make sense of it all."

"Hey," I jived, "maybe her letters are still with the top secret files that you and Hoberts—isn't it amazing how names stick with us—put in that public locker at Grand Central Station. Wasn't it that night when you both went on a bender?"

"Who could ever forget that!?" Dave chuckled. "Yeah, that would be a gas, her letters together with TRARG's top secret documents somewhere in the Pentagon catacombs. Intriguing, isn't it, that those files were retrieved from that station locker at Grand Central. Maybe I could file a Freedom of Information petition asking for both of them back!"

Mike sat peacefully, taking in the conversation. "Oh, God," she said teasingly, "I hope not. They were full of sexual turn-ons. I was always twitting Dave, playing to his fantasies, making up lots of stories."

"How much is a lot?" Dave asked sarcastically.

"Had I known," I cut in, "I would've asked him to let me read them, or at the very least, I would have riffled his foot locker bag." And I meant it.

"He's still into fantasies," she whispered leaning over, "but they've changed."

"How??" I feigned, "be specific, just the details, please."

"Well, now he dreams of weaving himself into one of his tapestries with nymphs prancing around him."

Dave took it all in. It was clear that their relationship had a long playful history, and I wondered how they had managed it against the odds.

But I couldn't take the banter a minute longer. "Enough. I've been waiting for this moment for a hell of a long time. What about Thule? What was it that impacted on us? I know you've given it thought. Enlighten me, please!"

Dave reached for the wine bottle and poured himself another glass. I got slightly nervous. "You're right. It's time we got into it. For me, Thule was the start of something deep within me. Partly it was the whole phantasmagoric setting, that tapestry of primitive designs and colors—but without the nymphs." He shot an impish glance at Mike. "It was all so elemental, so nitty-gritty. It was so damned serious, the Cold War on top of us.

"I remember being scared lots of times. Yeah, scared . . . I remember how often we prayed that nothing would happen, certainly not up in Thule. It was okay for the officers to get theirs but not us peons. Remember how often we toasted 'up yours' to Moscow Molly and her sidekick after she finished her broadcasts? Remember how often we prayed that they wouldn't extend our time, that we'd be out after our two year stint was up!"

Dave was just getting started. "But there was also a devil-may-care attitude. We were important but we were on short time. The irony was that we were the lowliest of the lowly, yet held key positions. They couldn't have done half of what was done without us, definitely the draftees. What I hated most was the propaganda. We knew the Soviets were up to no good but we also felt there was too much puffery, too much moralizing on our side.

"So when it came to my job, I took very seriously this order of the utmost secrecy of our mission. But the ineptitude, the corruption, the waste of money—it took away from the dedicated sense of it all.

"And as you know, now, looking back from this vantage point, it seems so foolish, the Russians no longer the enemy. All that money, billions upon billions, that could've gone to social programs—hell, just a tiny amount could've gone to support art programs in schools across the country. What a fucking waste!

"So, finally, what do I make of it? I think all of this makes for terrible contradictions. But wasn't this your line at the time? I'm just an artist, you're the historian. You were the one who spoke of entangling scenes, of reality and absurdity battling it out up there. And that unbelievable place, the Arctic, what could be more elemental than that!? As you used to say, this is the stuff of history."

For once, I didn't cut in. It was good hearing him expound again, recalling our walks at the height of night with the sun directly overhead, trekking around the fjords, sneaking across the low lying hills, or whispering across bunks in semi-darkness out of earshot of our tent-mates. "Can I add to what you've said, because I'm sure you know I always have something to add."

"That doesn't surprise me," he quipped.

I emptied the wine bottle into my glass. "Compared to my life since Thule, this episode was tiny, yet it's lasted a long time. Long, long, because in looking back I think of us as peculiar, bit-part actors in the theater of the Arctic. Yeah, we were on stage during this part of the Cold War. Not center stage—that was Korea—but close enough to the game to get good and scared every now and then. And close enough to get a perverse feel of what was strategically going on. What's more, we got paid, well, if you call $85 a month pay! That's got to be some kind of wild satisfaction in that.

"But after it was over, what did it all matter? It strikes me that the military gamble was an example of overkill. Thule, the massive air base, and TRARG, in its miniscule mission to figure out whether they could build yet another massive air base. To slay an enemy, does that require eliminating all boundaries??

"And then, right after we pulled out, Thule Air Base became virtually obsolete. Can you believe it? Once missiles were perfected, the bombers were no longer useful. We used to trek into places that they put the missiles. Instead of five hours to Moscow, now it's thirty-five minutes to targets. Even now they're poised and ready to launch! That's got to be the ultimate joke."

I took a deep breath, trying hard to unburden myself after all this time. "Well, the rollers think they won but I'm inclined to think that so much more was lost—money, energy, resources, and especially historical perspective. I remember that just about the same time came Michael Harrington's revelation in *The Other America* of the vast numbers of invisible poor that had multiplied all the while during Thule's construction and operation." A deep anger rolled in me, a sense of injustice and lost possibilities.

"Okay, Dave, now for the ultimate question, and I want an honest answer. No bullshitting."

"Shoot."

"You remember the endless discussions we had about the CID agent in our outfit, the only guy with top-top-secret status who reported directly back to the Washington about what was happening. It struck me that since you were in charge of intelligence, you were the one guy in a position to know who it was. Didn't you? Time to fess up."

"Yup."

"Bastard, and you refused to tell me all during that time. All right, who was it??"

Dave smiled and said simply, "Me."

I burst out laughing. "I don't for a minute believe you. Once again, you're holding back."

"Hell, Joe, it makes for a wonderful tapestry. I mean, this is where art and history come together, doesn't it, in one big wall-hanging showing life's contradictions. That was Thule, that was TRARG, and this is the end of the wine. So break out another bottle."

I did as told.

PART SIX

Ongoing Epilogue

The Past Never Quite Says Good-bye . . .

❄ ✪ ❄

Greenland: Inuits sue over U.S. base

Seventy-nine Inuits in Greenland have sued the Danish Government for being forced out of their homes when an American air base at Thule, a key installation in the cold war, was expanded in 1953. The Inuits are demanding $23.1 million for lost hunting grounds. (*New York Times*, 3 March 1998)

❄ ✪ ❄

Denmark: Apology to Inuits

Prime Minister Poul Nyrup Rasmussen apologized for the way his country forced Greenland Inuits out of their homes when a United States airbase was expanded in 1953. The apology, which Greenland has demanded for years, came after a Copenhagen court ruled the eviction was "serious infringement" on the rights of Greenland's indigenous people. (*New York Times*, 3 September 1999)

❄ ✪ ❄

Greenlanders wary of a new role in U.S. defenses

In mid-August, a group of former employees at Thule charged that the Pentagon has covered up the loss of a nuclear bomb from a B-52 bomber that crashed on sea ice seven miles from Thule on January 21, 1968. Based in Plattsburgh, N.Y., and loaded with four nuclear bombs, the airplane was flying over the area when it made an emergency crash landing, killing one crew member. (*New York Times*, 18 September 2000)

177

Study finds air route over North Pole feasible for flights to Asia
A joint Canadian–Russian study has found that opening air traffic routes over the North Pole, currently used by two or three flights a day, to thousands of commercial flights a year is "feasible and desirable."

Aviation experts said the study lays the groundwork for a huge increase in the number of flights across the Pole, and may make practical the first nonstop flights between such far-flung cities as New York, Bangkok or Singapore. (*New York Times*, 11 October 2000)

✳ ✪ ✳

Greenland base to be upgraded as part of missile shield plan
IGLIKU, Greenland. The United States, Denmark and Greenland signed agreements to upgrade the early warning radar systems at Thule, an important American air base during the cold war and now a crucial part of the Bush administration's plans for an antimissile defense system.

"Together we will meet the security challenges of the 21st century, from missile defense to international terrorism," Secretary of State Colin L. Powell said at a ceremony in this village. (*New York Times*, 1 August 2004, A4)

So does the past, so does Thule . . . endure . . .

NOTES

BIBLIOGRAPHY

Notes

Prologue II: Boston, 2011

1. David Halberstam, *The Coldest Winter: America and the Korean War* (New York: Hyperion, 2007), 632.

2. Bruce Cumings, *The Korean War: A History* (New York: Modern Library, 2010), xvii. "The Korean War is an unknown war because it transpired during the height of the McCarthy era (Julius and Ethel Rosenberg were indicted when the war began and executed just before it ended) making open inquiry and citizen dissent improbable" (79).

3. Mara Naselli, *Truth in Memoir*, Jan. 31, 2006, http:/identity theory.com/nonfiction/naselli_truth.php.

4. Robert L. Root Jr. and Michael J. Steinberg, *The Fourth Genre: The Contemporary Writers of/on Creative Nonfiction*, ed. 5 (White Plains, NY: Longman, 2010). Robert L. Root, "preserve experience" and Michele Morano. Quotes in panel discussion, "Travel in Nonfiction."

5. E. L. Doctorow, "False Documents," in *E. L. Doctorow: Essays and Conversations*, ed. Richard Trenner (Princeton: Ontario Review Press, 1983), 26. In this connection, the thoughts of Roland Barthes in "The Discourse of History" reverberate: "In the historical discourse of our civilization, the process of signification always aims at 'filling' the meaning of History: the historian is the one who collects not so much facts as signifies and relates them, i.e., organizes them in order to establish a positive meaning and to fill in the void of pure series." Roland Barthes, *The Rustle of Language*, trans. Richard Howard (Berkeley: University of California Press, 1986), 137–38.

6. Richard Hofstadter, *Anti-Intellectualism in American Life* (New York: Alfred A. Knopf, 1963), 3.

7. Quoted in Barbara Myerhoff, *Stories as Equipment for Living: Last Talks and Tales of Barbara Myerhoff*, ed. Marc Kaminsky and Mark Weiss, in collaboration with Deena Metzger (Ann Arbor: University of Michigan Press, 2007), 42.

1. Defying the Tundra: Dawn of a Base

1. Jean Malaurie, *The Last Kings of Thule* (George Allen and Unwin, 1956), 255–66.

2. Prisoners of Our Time

1. Joanna Kavenna, *The Ice Museum: In Search of the Lost Land of Thule* (New York: Viking Penguin, 2006), 2–5.

5. Ezekiel Saw the Wheel Way Up in Thule

1. "Birth of a Base: Now U.S. Can Be Told of the Huge Effort to Build 'Blue Jay' in Northern Greenland," *Life* 33, no. 12 (Sept. 22, 1952): 130–51.

10. The Bet atop the World

1. All things are indeed relative, particularly time and cost. A *New York Times* news story in mid-2010—"We All Scream at the Price of Ice Cream"—detailed the unimaginable, soaring cost of a single scoop of ice cream. Wrote Julia Moskin: "In Boston and Beverly Hills, not surprisingly, but also in Columbus, Ohio, and Arroyo Seco, N.M., a small cone or cup now often costs more than $4—and that's without the toppings of organic whipped cream, sustainable strawberries and French bittersweet chocolate chunks that also command dizzying prices" (4 Aug 2010, D1, 4.) Still, Mess Sergeant Gadget's magnificent ploy in Thule is tops in the history of ice cream and deserves a place in the *Guinness Book of World Records.*

11. Whirling Dervishes

1. Change inevitably occurs but some things remain steadfast: "From 85 feet up, the view of Coney Island is so good you can almost see the future . . . But I was in the front seat of the *Cyclone,* steadily ticking my way up to that first awful drop. I could see only doom. . . . The *Cyclone* car was starting to tip forward over the crest of that first hill, and I was about to die." Ariel Kaminer, "Thrilling Reminder of Old Coney Island: Shiny New Rides Replace Astroland but the *Cyclone*'s Rickety Glory Lives On," *New York Times,* 4 April 2010, 24.

Bibliography

Author's Files

Joseph Boskin. Diaries, letters, newsletters, notes, remembrances, 1952–1955.

Diaries/Interviews

Interview with Henry McIlwaine, TC 2nd LT. Conducted by Richard E. Killblane, historian, US Transportation Museum, Fort Eustis, Virginia, 2009.

Van Dommelen, David B. *North to the Past: A Greenland Experience.* Privately published, 1997.

Van Dommelen, David B., and Michal Van Dommelen. *Our Thumbs Were Young and Gay.* Unpublished memoir, 1951.

United States Government Documents

United States Army. Transportation Arctic Group, 9223rd Technical Services Unit, *Final Report.* Fort Eustis, Virginia, 1953.

Other Sources

Barthes, Roland. "The Discourse of History." In *The Rustle of Language,* translated by Richard Howard, 137–38. Berkeley: University of California Press, 1986.

"Birth of a Base: Now U.S. Can Be Told of the Huge Effort to Build 'Blue Jay' in Northern Greenland." *Life* 33, no. 12 (Sept. 22, 1952): 130–51.

Cumings, Bruce. *The Korean War: A History.* New York: Modern Library, 2010.

Doctorow, E. L. "False Documents." In *E. L. Doctorow: Essays and Conversations,* edited by Richard Trenner. Princeton: Ontario Review Press, 1983.

Halberstam, David. *The Coldest Winter: America and the Korean War.* New York: Hyperion, 2007.

Hofstadter, Richard. *Anti-Intellectualism in American Life.* New York: Alfred A. Knopf, 1963.

Kaminer, Ariel. "Thrilling Reminder of Old Coney Island: Shiny New Rides Replace Astroland but the *Cyclone*'s Rickety Glory Lives On." *New York Times,* 4 Apr. 2010, 24.

Kavenna, Joanna. *The Ice Museum: In Search of the Lost Land of Thule.* New York: Viking Penguin, 2006.

Malaurie, Jean. *The Last Kings of Thule.* London: George Allen and Unwin, 1956.

Moskin, Julia. "We All Scream at the Price of Ice Cream." *New York Times,* 4 Aug. 2010, D1, 4.

Myerhoff, Barbara. *Stories as Equipment for Living: Last Talks and Tales of Barbara Myerhoff.* Marc Kaminsky and Mark Weiss, eds. In collaboration with Deena Metzger. Ann Arbor: The Univ. of Michigan Press, 2007.

Naselli, Mara. "Truth in Memoir." Jan. 31, 2006. http://identitytheory.com/non fiction/naselli_truth.php.

Root, Robert L., Jr., and Michael J. Steinberg. *The Fourth Genre: The Contemporary Writers of/on Creative Nonfiction, ed. 5.* White Plains, NY: Longman, 2010.